2 week loan

Haynes Toddler Manual

Haynes, 2008

1844257371

Haynes

Toddler
Manual

Including extracts from
Haynes Baby Manual by Ian Banks (ISBN 978 1 84425 759 1)

Ian Banks

Cartoons by Jim Campbell

© Ian Banks 2008

Haynes Publishing
Sparkford, Yeovil, Somerset BA22 7JJ, England

Haynes North America, Inc
861 Lawrence Drive, Newbury Park, California 91320, USA

Haynes Publishing Nordiska AB
Box 1504, 751 45 Uppsala, Sweden

British Library Cataloguing in Publication Data:
A catalogue record for this book is available from the British Library

ISBN: 978 1 84425 737 9

Printed in Britain by J. H. Haynes & Co. Ltd., Sparkford.

The Author and the Publisher have taken care to ensure that the advice given in this edition is current at the time of publication. The Reader is advised to read and understand the instructions and information material included with all medicines recommended, and to consider carefully the appropriateness of any treatments. The Author and the Publisher will have no liability for adverse results, inappropriate or excessive use of the remedies offered in this book or their level of effectiveness in individual cases. The Author and the Publisher do not intend that this book be used as a substitute for medical advice. Advice from a medical practitioner should always be sought for any symptom or illness.

Contents

Foreword

Toddler books are not hard to find, but toddler manuals for men are about as thin on the ground as a good answer to 'where did I come from Daddy?' Even harder to get hold of is a parenting book which treats men as a valuable asset rather than a bolt-on extra. People wonder why, for instance, fathers either totally over-react to a toddler's illness or dismiss it as trivial. For many dads, there is no grey area in between. Now depending on your point of view this may be because men are inherently daft and incapable of looking after young children, or alternatively perhaps the lack of good male-friendly information could be a factor?

Toddler Manual follows Baby Manual just as night follows day, hair loss follows family holidays and toddlers follow mangy cats with malicious glee. Yes, dads may need their toddler to programme the DVD recorder. True, fathers are often seen wearing a look of grim determination as they approach supermarket checkouts with toddler-in-trolley. But this manual treats male parents with respect and recognition. With it you can deal with toddler tantrums, toddler temperatures, toddler travel and you don't always need to *whisper*!

Author's acknowledgements

Writing a toddler manual from memory alone is a recipe for disaster. Any dad ready to put pen to paper on such a subject must by definition have come through the other end. And memory can be very selective so people with more than a touch of objectivity can be vital. My thanks to my children Peter, Beth, John & Jen for giving me the practical experience and reminding me of the things gone hazy. Hilary, their mother, tries hard to make sure I can at least recall their dates of birth as we stand in front of very large and equally suspicious customs & immigration officials.

As with the Baby manual, I must also thank the organisations making such a difference to men as fathers, including Sure Start, the Men's Health Forum, the Family Planning Association and the British Medical Association. The fault-finding flow charts are based on material supplied by NHS Direct.

The people who make a manual into a book are artists. They include Ian Barnes, who did the editing and the picture research. Cartoonist Jim Campbell never grew up anyway so this one was pretty easy for him, and Matthew Minter has published so many books he must have a problem over their birth dates as well.

Dedication
To Augusta and Freya, who have probably taught their father enough to write his own manual by now.

How to get the best from your GP

Do your homework with our insider information

Surgery telephone lines will be busier at certain times of the day and week. When you make an appointment ask your practice receptionist about the best times to call to cancel your appointment should you need to.

Write down the symptoms before you see your doctor
- It is easy to forget the most important things during the examination. Doctors home-in on important clues. When did it start? Did anyone else suffer as well? Did this ever happen before? What have you done about it so far? Is the toddler on any medicines at present?

Arrive informed
- Check out the net for information before you go to the surgery. There are thousands of sites on health but many of them are of little real use. Click on NHS Direct as a start, or look in *Contacts* at the back of this book for up-to-date and accurate information.

Ask questions
- If a mechanic stuck his head into the bonnet of your car you would most certainly want to know what he intended. This doctor is about to lift the lid on your child's body. Don't be afraid to ask questions about what a test will show, how a particular treatment works, and when you should come back.

Don't beat around the bush
- With an average of only seven minutes for each consultation it's important to get to the point.

Listen to what the doctor says
- If you don't understand, say so. It helps if they write down the important points. Most people pick up less than half of what their doctor has told them.

Have your prescription explained
- Make sure you know what it is for. Are there any side effects you should look out for?

If you want a second opinion say so
- Ask for a consultant appointment by all means but remember you are dealing with a person with feelings and not a computer. Compliment him for his attention first but then explain your deep anxiety.

Flattery will get you anywhere
- Praise is thin on the ground these days. An acknowledgment of a good effort, even if not successful, will be remembered.

Be courteous with all the staff
- Receptionists are not dragons trying to prevent you seeing a doctor. Practice nurses increasingly influence your treatment. General practice is a team effort and you will get the best out of it by treating all its members with respect.

Be prepared to complain
● If possible see your doctor first and explain what is annoying you. Family doctors now have an 'in-house' complaints system, and most issues are successfully resolved at this level. If you are still not satisfied you can take it to a formal hearing.

Trust your doctor
● There is a difference between trust and blind faith. Your health is a partnership between you and your doctor where you are the majority stakeholder.

Change your GP with caution
● Thousands of people change their doctor each year. Most of them have simply moved house. You do not need to tell your family doctor if you wish to leave their practice. Your new doctor will arrange for all your notes to be transferred. The whole point of general practice is to build up a personal insight into the health of you and your family. A new doctor has to start almost from scratch.

Don't be afraid to ask to see your notes
● You have the right to see what your doctor writes about you. Unfortunately doctors' language can be difficult to understand. Latin and Greek are still in use although on the decline. Doctors use abbreviations in your notes. Watch out for:

a) TATT: An abbreviation for Tired All The Time.
b) TCA SOS: To Call Again if things get worse. Most illnesses are self-limiting. A couple of weeks usually allows nature to sort things out.
c) RV: Review. Secretaries will automatically arrange a subsequent appointment.
d) PEARLA: Pupils Equal and Reacting to Light and Accommodation. A standard entry on a casualty sheet to show that your brain is functioning.
e) RTA: Road Traffic Accident.
f) FROM: Full Range Of Movement at a joint.
g) SOB: Short Of Breath. If this comes on after walking in from the waiting room it turns into SOBOE – On Exercise.
h) AMA/CMA: Against Medical Advice/Contrary Medical Advice: You went home despite medical advice not to do so.
i) DNA: Did Not Attend. You didn't turn up for your appointment.
j) SUPRATENTORIAL: If your doctor thinks you are deluding yourself over your symptoms and it's really all in your head, he might think the problem lies above (supra) your tentorium. Rarely used these days.
k) HYSTERIA: A dangerous diagnosis. In essence your doctor believes you are possibly over-dramatising the situation. Rarely used these days.

Home medicine chest

Minor illnesses or accidents can happen at any time so it's worth being prepared. It makes sense to keep some first aid and simple remedies in a safe place in the house to cover most minor ailments and accidents. The picture shows an example of a well stocked and maintained kit. Ask your pharmacist for advice on which products are best.

- Painkillers.
- Anti-diarrhoeal, rehydration mixture.
- Indigestion remedy, eg antacids.
- Travel sickness tablets.
- Sunscreen – SPF15 or higher.
- Sunburn treatment.
- Tweezers, sharp scissors.
- Thermometer.
- A selection of plasters, cotton wool, elastic bandages and assorted dressings.

Remember
- Keep the medicine chest in a secure, locked place, out of reach of small children.
- Do not keep in the bathroom as the damp will soon damage the medicines and bandages.
- Always read the instructions and use the right dose.
- Watch expiry dates – don't keep or use medicines past their sell-by date.

Home medicine kit

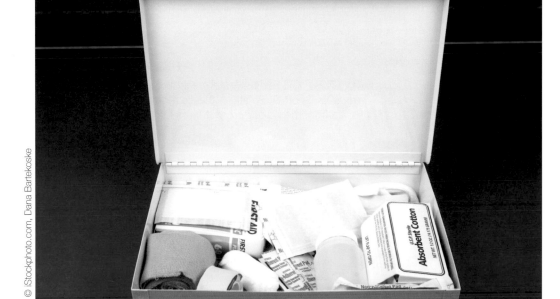

Photo: © iStockphoto.com, Dana Bartekoske

1

PART

Introduction

Dad's time

Babies discover dads at roughly the same time babies turn into human beings and male human beings turn into dads. Pre-toddler they are much more interested in what mum can deliver on demand than this hairy face with stubble like Desperate Dan. Babies' skin does not respond well to cheeks resembling a wire brush, although great for cleaning the BBQ.

Not only is mum softer and less abrasive, she can miraculously produce milk and it's not even pasteurised. Growing awareness of another person important in your life starts to kick in around the time communication is less concerned with feeding and driven more by curiosity. 'Who is this huge person and why does he keep pulling my toes one by one?' At the same time dads waiting in the wings suddenly find inquisitive eyes and ears turning in their direction. For many dads this is the most exciting time of fatherhood. A helping hand is always welcome so long as it is neither patronising or judgmental.

> Wrinkles are hereditary. Parents get them from their children.
> **Doris Day**

Photo: © iStockphoto.com

If you buy a car manual you expect the writer to be an expert at fixing cars. There is no shortage of 'experts' in parenting although the vast majority of parent manuals are written by women for mothers. Manuals for dads are relatively thin on the ground despite the increasing number of men staying at home looking after the children. Experts are also expected to do what they preach. When I watch certain TV motoring programmes I do sometimes wonder. Parenting is different. I will be the first to admit that there were times when I lost my cool with our four children and would have been glad to have something like this manual to beat them about the head and neck with. Being there is always more important than simply reading about it. Not whacking your kids is always easier when there are some alternatives to try first. With each successive child I went from being a firm believer in giving bum whacks to giving none. Our last two kids never experienced what many would consider perfectly normal, indeed desirable for discipline. They were no more or less misbehaved than their older brother and sister. The difference was in us as parents, we were better able to cope in so many other ways as well simply from having been there. This manual is no replacement for learning the hard way and doesn't pretend to be, but maintaining a car is more than a tad different from bringing up children, keeping them safe while allowing them to learn from their own mistakes. Cars are replaceable. Even so, knowing some tricks of the trade and that you are not alone can help keep your hair on. Well most of it anyway.

You have a lot of fun coming your way Toddler Dad, your laughs will outnumber the tears even though it might not seem like that at times.

PART **1**

INTRODUCTION

What about dad?

Nobody doubts being a father can often be great fun and really rewarding but it can also be stressful and demanding. Toddler time is measured by the bucket and dad's own feelings can get lost in the hectic schedule of balancing home/work/toddler.

Having a range of different feelings is natural, they come and go varying in strength depending on the situation. The trick as a toddler dad is to be aware of these feelings and recognise when they are getting out of hand. Toddlers are very aware of how their parents feel, even without saying anything about it and this can affect them and their behaviour.

What a dad feels depends on lots of things:
- Personality and temperament.
- Support, or lack of it, from a partner, family and friends.
- The number, age and health of other children.
- Working full or part-time.
- Concerns over money (hands up, which toddler dad is *not* concerned over money?).
- Quality of home/accommodation.
- Camel straws such as a separation, a bereavement or unemployment.
- Childhood experiences and how well they were coped with.

Photo: © iStockphoto.com, Dagmar Heymans

Easy to say but obviously an important part of being a dad is the ability to be sensitive and responsive to a toddler's emotions. Children experience and express strong emotions and that can sometimes be challenging for a dad. Traditionally men were brought up to deny the full range of their feelings, and can be surprised at how powerfully they can come back when bringing up their own children. Not surprisingly there may be times when dads struggle with difficult feelings such as:

- Anger.
- Resentment.
- Exhaustion.
- Envy.
- Boredom.
- Guilt.
- Sadness.
- Disappointment.
- Despair.

Although it can be painful to acknowledge the more negative feelings, it is helpful to try and make sense of how to react, not least to make sure dads can look after themselves and enjoy the good aspects of being a parent.

Childhood memories of being treated badly by parents can flavour a relationship with a toddler unless the memories are used to avoid doing exactly the same thing. A good example is temper control or rather losing it. It can take a conscious effort not to make the same mistake.

All this stuff is great in theory but oh boy, how I wish I could look in the mirror and say 'well done'. In truth there's no such thing as a perfect dad, we all have good and bad days and will all make mistakes.

Dad development

It's not just the kids who go though stages of development, dads experience needs as a parent and this will change over time depending on the age and developmental stage of the children.

What matters is to realise that it's ok to feel in need of help at times. So for instance after the birth, dads as well as mums need time, support and encouragement to develop bonds with their child.

Getting involved is the key and while being put off at times by comments such as, 'Look, you're doing it all wrong, this is the way to hold a baby', men are every bit as able to look after kids as women. It's important to recognise that whilst it's healthy to have a bit of space now and then from the child, becoming distant or withdrawing physically and emotionally isn't going to help dads in the long run.

Dads once removed

Need help? Grandparents can often be a great source of commonsense advice. So OK they often focus in on the toddler

and not the dad but that's natural. Toddlers on board means that everyone has to adjust their place and position in the family. Dad's knee sometimes has to be shared and this can be quite painful sometimes.

Conflicting relationships

At some point there will come a clash of priority with often painful feelings around how close the bond is between your child and the mother of the child. When the child is very young, you may feel quite left out, and begin to wonder when you'll be able to bond with your child in the way that your partner has. Worry not mate, your time will come and yet, despite these feelings, your partner will probably be expecting a lot of support from you. Going out to work can make it all the more difficult and the fact you can't see your daughter or son during the day may increase the danger of getting angry or seeming not to be interested.

Second opinion

Don't be in the least bit surprised if you and your partner have different views at times about how to be a parent. This can lead to rows and unhappiness if you find that you are often at odds. However, it's worth remembering that no one way of parenting is always 'right', and that your opinions about how best to do things are as important as anyone else's.

A young child will look to its parents as role models. A dad who is capable of managing his emotions, being able to deal with his own anger, for example, by keeping things together, and not yelling or shouting; or being able to admit to feelings of disappointment or frustration, rather than bottling them up, and denying them, will provide his son or daughter with a really helpful example of how to be a mature person who can understand and deal with the range of feelings that come about during the course of everyday life. Dead easy toddler dad… easier said than done.

Dads in lieu

As a step-father to a child or a number of children most if not all of this advice works for you too. You may have particular stresses. For example, it can be very painful if you feel that your partner's children are rejecting you, particularly when you are going out of your way to get along with them. Your step-children have probably been through some sad and distressing times and may be missing their biological father. Perhaps they feel they are being disloyal to their father if they are friendly with you. It's bound to be a very complex situation which needs a lot of time and patience to settle down, and one which may well demand a lot from you in terms of your ability to remain positive, even in the face of anger and resentment. You may also need to reassure any children you may have from a previous relationship that you still love them and will always be their father.

You may feel disappointed that you don't get to spend as much time alone with your partner as you would like and find yourself resenting your step-children. It's not uncommon to have these kind of feelings and it may be a good idea to talk to your partner about how you're feeling and how difficult the situation can be. Taking the time to talk this through with your partner and children is vital.

Photo: © iStockphoto.com

2

PART

What to expect

PART ② Child development

Contrary to constant desire for standardisation, there is no such thing as 'normal development'. In terms of weight gain, behavioural changes, speech and walking there are only averages and all children develop at different rates, attaining skills at different ages. Being 'slow' to walk is not a sign of poor development. Similarly 'delayed' speech is not a sign of impaired intellect. You should consider all the various milestones and discuss them with your health visitor.

One year

Movement and posture.	● May stand alone for a few seconds and may walk with assistance. ● Can sit itself up from lying down and will sit for indefinite periods on the floor playing happily ● Will crawl on hands and knees and can move quite rapidly. ● Is fully able to pull itself to a standing position and lay itself down again.
Eyes and responses.	● Now holding an object in each hand, knocking them together. ● Drops and throws deliberately to see what happens and points at wanted objects. ● Often recognises known faces the other side of the room. ● Possibly able to show preference in using right or left hand.
Play.	● Shows pleasure in seeing familiar faces. ● Finds toys if they are totally hidden while it is watching. ● Prefers and seeks toys that make a sound. ● Hands toys to parents and release them by opening the hand. ● Plays pat-a-cake and waves bye-bye. ● Drinks well from normal cup and will hold out arms and legs for dressing. ● Tries to ring toy bell by shaking it if shown how to do it.
Speech.	● Speech-like sounds taking inflection and form. ● Parents will be able to recognise from 2 to 6 words that the baby says. ● Can understand simple instruction like, 'Give it to mummy.' ● Knows and responds to own name. ● Understands a number of words, such as ball, cup and spoon.

Photo: © iStockphoto.com, Rebecca Ellis

18 months

Movement and posture.
- Often carries a favourite toy such as a teddy bear by an arm or leg.
- Now walks upstairs with assistance, but not downstairs.
- Now playing and picking up toys.
- Might walk alone, both starting and stopping without falling and may run, but is stopped by obstacles.

Eyes and responses.
- Finger grasp now more subtle, can pick up pins and can hold a pencil quite simply.
- Points at distant objects.
- Turning pages of a book.
- Recognises previously seen books and contents.
- Builds a tower of 3 cubes.

Speech.
- Can now use and understand around 20 words and enjoys nursery rhymes.
- Understands and will point to hair, nose, feet and hands.
- Likes singing.
- 'Talks' loudly and continuously while playing.
- Will follow spoken instructions.

Mind changes

Expensive toys are the quick way out when it comes to stimulating your child's brain to think. Sadly they are often not very good either. Computer games are now discouraged for children under 7 years. In truth, you don't need expensive toys to help your child learn. Instead, you can teach them through playing, singing, reading and talking.

Talking

When it comes to stimulating your child's mind, the most important thing is talking with your toddler all the time even when they cannot answer in any form of recognisable language.

At around 12 months babies start to take an interest in language and understand what individual words mean.

At around 15 months you'll usually hear your child's first word. But by two years old they should have a range of single words and many children will be talking in short sentences.

Baby talk?

Gently pushing them with vocabulary can start at an early age. it's really important that you talk to children not just about concrete things but about subtler concepts. Descriptive terms are useful in widening their view of life and concept of their own environment. Being a big person or the fire being red hot adds colour to their world of speech. Speaking numbers also helps: two teddies, three bananas or one glass of milk gets them ready to recognise multiples of what they are looking at.

If your toddler replies in single sentences reply in two, if two then try three. You will gradually get them used to holding a conversation rather than simply grunting in all the right places.

2 years 6 months

Eyes and responses.
- Recognises a picture of self.
- Attentive to small detail in pictures.
- Can build a tower of 6-8 cubes/blocks using one hand and can usually draw a circle.
- Draw a vertical line when shown.
- Wash own hands.
- Eating and drinking successfully with spoon.
- Usually dry through night and can pull down pants for toilet.
- May throw a tantrum when restrained.

Play.
- May watch other children play but not necessarily join in.
- Playing for long periods with toys but still requires parents' attention.

Speech.
- Possibly hold a conversation of a few sentences.
- Use prepositions.

3 years

Responses.
- Identify 4 pictures naming the people in them or what it is showing.
- Identify a family friend by name.
- Be understood and less likely to throw a tantrum when not.
- Dress themselves to a varying degree, but don't expect a finished result.
- Make their own breakfast so long as it is a slice of bread or bowl of cereal.

Play.
- Throw balls both under and overhand.
- Joins in with play more often than not.

Speech.
- Starts using adjectives.

PART ② Immunisation

Childhood immunisation is one of the main reasons we have eradicated many childhood diseases in this country. By boosting your child's immune response they can fight infections which once killed or maimed countless millions of children.

Polio is now history and measles no longer infects children in the USA. The EU aims to eradicate measles and rubella (German Measles) within the next decade or so. Some children will be left less protected because they:

● Cannot be immunised for medical reasons.
● Cannot get to the vaccine services.
● Are one of the few where the vaccine doesn't work.

If enough children are vaccinated this will not matter as the 'herd' immunity will prevent the spread of infection.

Even the so-called common childhood conditions such as whooping cough can kill. It is therefore very important to protect children from these diseases.

Despite much media attention there is still no definite link proven between the triple vaccine MMR with either Crohn's disease or autism. Using the vaccine separately is possible but

Photo: © iStockphoto.com, Mikhail Tolstoy

is less effective than the combined injection and does, of course, triple the number of injections required for full protection. In those countries where the MMR uptake has declined there has been a corresponding increase in the number of measles cases. If you are concerned about having your child immunised, contact your health visitor to discuss your concerns.

Serious reactions to the vaccination are rare but inflammation and itchness at the injections site is common as is a temporary fever. Child preparations of paracetamol or ibuprofen can help (always read the label first).

If you miss a vaccination appointment, you do not have to start the course of vaccines again. The recommended gap between vaccines is an ideal – if you miss one, just make a new appointment as soon as you can.

The following is a guide to the recommended timetable for immunisations.

Age	Immunisation (vaccine given)
2 months	**DTP/Polio/Hib** (Diphtheria, Tetanus, Pertussis, Polio, and Haemophilus Influenza B) all in one injection, plus: **Pneumococcal (PCV)** in a separate injection
3 months	**DTP/Polio/Hib** (2nd dose), plus: **MenC (Meningococcus Group C)** in a separate injection
4 months	**DTP/Polio/Hib** (3rd dose), plus: **MenC** (2nd dose) in a separate injection, plus: **Pneumococcal (PCV)** (2nd dose) in a separate injection
Around 12 months	**Hib/MenC** (combined as one injection - 4th dose of Hib and 3rd dose of MenC)
Around 13 months	**MMR** (Measles, Mumps and Rubella combined as one injection), plus: **Pneumococcal (PCV)** (3rd dose) in a separate injection
Around 4-5 years	'Pre-school' booster of **DTP/Polio**, plus: **MMR** (second dose) in a separate injection
Around 13-18 years	**Td/Polio** booster. (A combined injection of Tetanus, low dose Diphtheria, and Polio.)
Adults	**Influenza and Pneumococcal** if you are aged 65 or over **Td/Polio** - at any age if you were not fully immunised as a child

Note
DTP, Polio and Hib vaccines are combined into one injection - the DTP/Polio/Hib vaccine.

Pneumococcal (PCV) is a separate injection and was added to the routine immunisation schedule in September 2006.

> **Do multiple vaccines overload the toddler's immune system?**
> No. Toddlers are exposed to more challenges to their immune system every day in the environment around them than from all of the vaccines contained in the routine immunisation schedule put together.

Meningococcus group C vaccine (MenC) is sometimes given as a separate injection but is combined with Hib for one injection.

Td/Polio is Tetanus, low dose Diphtheria and Polio vaccines combined as one injection.

Polio immunisation changed in 2004. The polio vaccine is now combined with DPT/Hib or Td and given by injection. It used to be given by mouth (oral vaccine) as a few drops of vaccine on the tongue. If you have previously started a course of polio immunisation with oral vaccine you can finish off the course with polio injections. You do not need to start again.

Measles, mumps and rubella vaccines are combined into one injection - the MMR vaccine.

Common adverse reactions
● Swelling, redness, soreness at the injection site.
● Slightly raised temperature (lower than 39°C/102.2°F).
● Restlessness or generally feeling 'off-colour'

Measles, mumps and rubella (MMR)
It is not unusual for a rash to appear 7 to 10 days after the injection; the child may seem unwell during this time. See *Measles* and *German measles* self care sections for advice (see pages 173 and 175).

Polio vaccine
As this vaccine is known to be excreted, care must be taken to wash hands thoroughly after changing a baby's nappy following this vaccination.

Self care
● The above symptoms should be short-lived.
● Ensure the toddler is not overdressed. A vest and nappy/pants is enough as long as the house is at normal room temperature.
● Cover the toddler in a light cotton sheet when in bed.
● Give paracetamol to reduce temperature. Check instructions on packet for right dose.
● If the soreness at the injection site is bigger than a 10p coin, and spreading over the arm/leg, the toddler may need to be seen by a health professional. Phone NHS Direct (see *Contacts* on page 183) for further advice and information.

If you have any other concerns, get in touch with your health visitor, a practice nurse, NHS Direct or a general practitioner.

Further information
If you would like to know more, contact NHS Direct or look in the *Contacts* section at the back of this manual.

PART

Bonding and communication

Mum's the word. It certainly is if you are 3 weeks old and breast-fed. Dads are people who give great hugs but are a bit short on the goodies. Babies have little contact with their father in the early days. Awareness of there being _two_ important people in their lives arrives slowly with time. Dads are usually waiting in the wings.

While it is true that children become aware of their fathers gradually, it can be said that some dads do the same thing with regard to their new baby. It is a reflection of just how powerful a simple show of affection can be, that as the child grows they are prepared to leave the arms of their source of food, their breast-feeding mother, for those of their father. It has to be said that all of ours did a quick check to make sure mum hadn't nipped off permanently, before chewing contentedly on my nose. Cuddle quality is important. In experiments on animal behaviour, baby chimps will favour a warm, hairy dummy with no milk, to a cold, smooth dummy milk supply. The chimps spent their time between both, using the non-hairy dummy simply as a supply of food.

What is important from these intimacies is not just the ability to talk, feed or play. It is the effect each has on the bond which

Photo: © iStockphoto.com

Being a fairly tense sort of person, I was a mug for all the 'stress' toys which you squeeze, punch or otherwise abuse to let off steam. When my daughter came along, I found the perfect 'stress release'. A cuddle always did the trick, I'm sure she has stopped me having a heart attack!

New father

There is evidence that having something to cuddle, even a cat or dog, prolongs life. This is supported by statistics which show that men in stable partnerships with children live longer on average than single men with no children.

develops between a very young person and an older one. Fathers have an uphill struggle against what is expected of them. A steep learning curve is involved with little to go on except what has been traditionally performed by mothers. Innovation is the key as we have everything to gain from experimentation.

Talking

Most men say their relationship with their child really takes off once they start talking. New men will dispute this and say it is only the way society used to expect fathers to relate to their children. Indeed many men now insist on being involved at an early stage in the development of language. Talking, if we mean communication, actually takes place very soon after birth. Babies indicate what they want very effectively by using their voice. Mothers can tell the often subtle difference between cries indicating the demand for food to that of wanting attention. Fathers are also able to do so, but usually later on. Conversation also takes place. Inflections in voice, along with the urgency with which it is spoken by the baby, convey a great deal of information. Some babies respond to loud talking, others to soft gentle speech. This may reflect the amount of 'background' noise in the home but may also be an expression of their own personality. From this type of contact we very quickly learn what babies like in the style of conversation. Admittedly much of the conversation is one-way.

Fashion changes between generations on the style which should be used when speaking to a baby. Modernists reject 'baby talk' and insist that we speak to them as miniature adults. Traditionalists say this is useless and robs the child of the intimacy of such talk. It is interesting that much of 'love talk' between adults would fail a test of good English. Studies on eye contact between babies and parents show that the constant emphasis on changes in tonal inflection of speech maintains interest. Speech of whatever form which maintains a constant pitch does not have the same attraction to babies. Rhetoric is probably appreciated at a very early age and as all politicians know well, on occasion it is not what you say that counts, but how you say it.

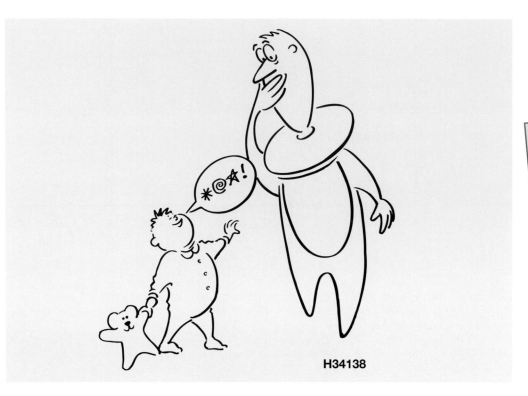

H34138

Children are constantly picking up conversation not directed at themselves . . .

All toddlers probably get a mixture of both as they are constantly picking up conversation not directed to themselves. This is manifested by children suddenly repeating a phrase or word which most certainly would not have been for their ears. Children will always wait until they are in the most genteel company of adoring aunts before making these utterances. Most groups of researchers are agreed upon one thing: babies adore repetition, especially in speech. Telling or singing the same nursery rhyme may be boring to you, but to your baby it is a recognisable pattern in an otherwise chaotic world. Even as they grow older the desire for repeatability remains and reading the same story over again becomes par for the course. Children will allow a certain amount of variation on the theme but the basic structure has to remain the same. It is the gentle nuances in speech which introduces variation. If this appears unlikely, it is worth remembering the impact of constantly sung football or rugby songs. Adult men find security in the predictable chant as do their children. It is the group involvement which supplies the confidence. Singing a nursery rhyme for the 100th time conveys commitment and security. Experimentation is the name of the game, so long as it is within certain boundaries of familiarity.

Catch 22

From baby to toddler it is important for your child to become accustomed to your voice. It is obviously through this route that lies the major stimulus to make noises which will eventually result in speech. Babies are already exposed to their mother's speech while in the womb. This is reinforced by intimate contact after being born. It may well be that it is for this reason that babies are often little disturbed by a mother's sneeze or cough. There exists for men, therefore, a Catch 22. Men have not only traditionally been slow to talk to their babies or toddlers, possibly through self-consciousness, but they have had less opportunity to

Photo: © iStockphoto.com, Yvonne Chamberlain

do so. Many men leave for work while their children are in bed and return from work to find them in the same place. Despite the changes which are taking place in work patterns, men in the UK still work the longest hours in the EU, so for all these reasons, and more besides, the baby learns and becomes accustomed to the father's voice after that of the mother's. A similar thing happens to face recognition. Not talking regularly to a baby will make them fretful when you do, which can set up a vicious cycle where the father's attempts at communication are met with crying which discourages him from trying again, which makes it even worse the next time he does try. While there are no easy answers, the use of 'quality' time, when a father does have the opportunity to hold and talk to his children, is vital even if it is confined to brief periods.

Brain power

It is incredible how the human brain not only learns a language but even learns to speak in the first place. Frustration is written all over the face of a toddler who can understand speech but its brain has not yet worked out how to actually speak. A similar but more devastating phenomenon occurs with the adult brain which has been damaged by stroke. A common result of such injury is the ability of the person to recognise an object but be unable to state its name. Thus a watch becomes 'time' or 'day'. Such is the frustration for people thus afflicted they will often substitute a string of expletives which can be startling in their clarity compared to the hesitant inaccurate speech of which they are normally capable. Babies and toddlers demonstrate the same frustration and will become impatient when you fail to understand that the unintelligible collection of consonants they are hurling at you at top volume simply means 'I want a biscuit'. Interestingly, they will often treat the adult as an idiot and turn to one of their older siblings to act as an interpreter who promptly says, with just a touch of superiority, 'He wants a biscuit daddy'. When all else fails on the language front, babies and young toddlers will simply point a finger until *you* get it right. This can lead to a crescendo of frustration both from the child, who patently considers the father an idiot, and the father who simply *feels* like an idiot. Part of the pleasure of fatherhood is getting the pointing finger correct and being able to say the name of the object of desire. Like many facets of parenthood it is usually short-lived as your child recognises a way of maintaining attention even when there is no immediate object of desire. The pointing finger is truly a powerful tool in learning the name of things.

Helping them to talk

Attempts at talking at an early age depends to large extent on the amount of stimulation you provide. The ability to experiment with words and language will determine how well your child will cope with many other facets of learning later on in their development. Without doubt, some fathers find talking to a baby or even a toddler very difficult. Often these dads will also find small talk difficult, and would prefer to say nothing than talk just for the sake of it. If you are like this, and you are in the majority of dads, it can help to set up situations which make such conversation easier.

Dressing

Babies and toddlers are fascinated by clothes. It helps you if you 'talk them down' when taking off all the various garments. The same thing happens when putting them back on again. Baby-grows can produce a most stimulating conversation, as there always appears to be one press-stud too many. Now is the time to practise expletive-free conversation. Feeding is a similar opportunity for conversation, you won't be the first father to explain that the rapidly approaching spoonful of baby food is in fact a train about to enter a tunnel.

Picture books

A time-honoured way of promoting interaction. You supply the commentary and pointing finger, they supply the laughs and

impatience to see the next page even though you are only half way through this one. Don't underestimate what is going in during these sessions. Many a toddler will let you know very quickly if you have turned the page before they have digested the previous one completely. Memory in a young child is uncluttered with telephone numbers, useless facts and dates. They have plenty of room, therefore, for what you said the last time you went through a particular story. Going too fast and skipping large chunks will be noticed by your child who will not be slow to let you know what they think of the present service.

Question-time

Conversations should be two way. Asking questions like 'Did you like that?' may not produce definitive answers but you may be rewarded by a gleeful shout. Remember to answer their questions as well. They may not sound like questions but any response is better than none. Avoid answering your own questions too often and allow them time to make their verbal or non-verbal response.

It's not just what you say

Toddlers will be just as fascinated by the latest political scandal as by *Blue Peter*. It is more the attention given along with the intonation which will delight your child.

Milestones of development

Being involved as a father is not only important to your child, it is important for your memories of how they grew up. The fun comes from listening out for the stages of language development. A mixture of pleasure and fear, listening to a child experiment with words raises apprehension over the speed of their development. Medical text books will lay down milestones through which the child should pass during normal development. These indicators of 'normal' development can be a source of constant worry for the parents of completely normal children who fail to meet the 'deadline' on time. Failure to build a tower of four bricks can be endured but a failure to talk is often seen as a real disaster and portends failure in society. If these books are read carefully they will explain that 'normality' is not only impossible to define but that it is also undesirable when talking about human beings of whatever age. Most doctors happily settle for the average age at which a milestone will be reached with the sure knowledge that there will be children who are a little above or below this average yet will be as 'normal' as the next child.

Teachers and health visitors are probably better people to talk to than doctors over this issue of child development, and they will agree with the medical profession that children have different rates of development in different areas. One of our children was slow to perfect their speech and was borderline for help from the speech therapist, a specialist in speech development. They were also however, adept at experimentation with language and would use it to produce the greatest response for their demands rather than praise for grammatical correctness. Your health visitor will give good advice with regard to the speed of your child's speech development.

Bite your tongue

Allow some mistakes in their speech. Constant correction will impede experimentation. Nursery rhymes, songs and chants are all good ways of instilling confidence in a child in the use of language and do not need to be in BBC English. Patience and encouragement will pay great dividends when your child first tries to tell a story, and will allow them to develop their expression through language. The energetic use of language to convey a message, which is why it was invented in the first place, is more important in the early stages than its grammatical accuracy. Exactly *when* they start is less important than *how*. This timing can be influenced by the presence or absence of other children. If a child can get by with expressions and body language easily interpreted by siblings, it may reduce the stimulus for talking. Alternatively, the intimate and often sustained contact with their brothers and sisters who are talking, increases the exposure to speech. All our children began to use speech at different times and this had little if any reflection on their ability at school or as part of our family.

With five children it was easy to see a pattern. Our eldest started speaking first, and with each successive child the delay got greater. They were finding that they did not have to use spoken language to communicate for what they wanted.

Father of five

This is not always the way for all children. For some the stimulus of other children talking seems to trigger their own use of speech.

First words

Whether a baby says 'da da' or 'ma ma' is always disputed as first words. It is not the word which counts, rather than the response it will evoke. Few words will come out perfectly first time and are at best a phonetic approximation. Commonly there is little if any relationship between the word as pronounced by the baby and the object of their desire. What is interesting is how the phonetic inaccuracies of their siblings are forced upon later children. This can even descend from previous generations and become established as 'first words' for the new child. Unconsciously these mispronunciations are fed back to the child as a form of reinforcement so that they recognise only the 'baby' equivalent. Thus a bottle becomes a *bo bo*. A similar and long standing teaching method occurs with phonetic teaching where letters of the alphabet take on their phonetic sounds. Ah, Buh, Cuh, etc, can be considered an extension of the baby talk which was once called 'mother tongue'. Part of the fun of having children may well revolve around the use of grammatically incorrect language as witnessed by the chuckles they can produce in the adult population. Like Father Christmas and Peter Pan, it may be part of a desire to preserve the state of childhood for as long as possible.

Play

Play is important. It is different from a game which implies rules. Play is a great leveller bringing both toddler and father to the same plane of simply having *fun*. Without doubt there may be an unconscious attempt to teach and learn, but as a bond, for a brief spell, baby and father are united in warmth and need no language. Given that play appears to have constructive value it is surprising that it tends to be delegated to people who 'have more free time'. This is the equivalent of growing a prize melon but letting someone else eat it. Play is a learning experience. It not only develops ability at art or construction, it also builds confidence, promotes sharing and even allows children to teach other children without them realising what they are doing. More important for fathers, it is a tax-free way of blowing off steam, doing something just because it is *fun*. The paradox is that play with your child can be hard work. Even so there are ways of limiting the effort and increasing the pleasure.

Avoid invoking rules for play with very young children. They will develop their own rules, which like politician's oaths, tend to be flexible.

Stories and plays

Toddlers love stories and plays. It is part of getting ready for real life. They particularly like to act out what they hear and make up. Puppets, and these can be as simple as socks or ice lolly sticks tied together, provide a material basis for their imagination. Older toddlers tend to direct; like the younger ones, you should be content to supply ideas and be the bad guy.

Painting

Painting comes naturally when young. Unfortunately young people tend to paint everything except the paper. Getting upset over the mess is about as useful as Canute opposing the next tide. Invest in a large sheet of plastic floor covering and sacks of brushes, paint and child-safe felt-tip pens.

> *Our table invariably ends up like a Salvador Dali creation. Polyurethane varnish is truly a wonderful invention!*
> **Father of five**

Imagination

Storytelling need not be straight from a book. Develop a theme such as 'islands to be ship-wrecked on', or 'tunnels that lead to…'. You only need to provide the canvas, they will supply the paint. Imagination is more powerful than any printer's ink.

The force of gravity

Children, like Newtonian apples, will always return to Earth. Children, however, have yet to be taught this basic fact of physics and consider it quite normal to be attached to their father's anatomy even when he is trying to use the toilet. Most men very soon realise that it is always easier to sit down rather than try the single handed approach, no matter how accustomed they are to journeys by train. As they slip inexorably lower down mum, they would be stopped by a hip, mum's hod-carrier. Unfortunately for men, nothing can halt this downward slide until a little heap of person is clutching a pair of knees.

Strongman act

There are some advantages in being the father. You are perceived, rightly or wrongly, as being stronger and you will often get away with more 'rough' play than your partner. Allowing them to ride around on your foot, having slipped all the way down from your chest, may not be particularly comfortable, but it is awesome to a child and probably stops your blood vessels furring up.

> *Coming home tired, the last thing I want to do is play wrestling on the carpet. Yet once it starts I feel refreshed. Perhaps it is just so different from my daily grind at the desk.*
> **Father of one child**

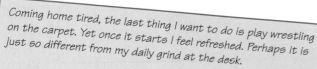

Bonding through feeding

To feed a person, toddler or otherwise, establishes a bond, the significance of which is never lost between both parties. Watching someone eat and enjoy their food is part of human contact and is the basis of many 'food' programmes on the TV. Many chefs, male and female, will admit that they enjoy preparing food and watching other people eat more than eating the food themselves. Watching your own child feed is even more special and you will be assured of 'many happy returns'.

Food from dad's plate *always* tastes better than your own. My father used to 'sneak' in the bone from the Sunday joint as if this was some major war-time success of the commandos. Three children fell upon this offering as though it was the first food seen since Adam bit a Cox's Pippin. Ask us to eat up the meat on our plates however, and everyone was just too full for even one more bite, cake being the only exception to the rule. What was interesting was the acceptance that my father had somehow 'stolen' the bone from the gaze of my mother. The forbidden fruit indeed, and this demonstrated a fundamental grasp of the concept when trying to feed children. This same game would be played out between mother and father with secretive pleadings of 'you can have this *but don't tell your father'*. Children desperately want unity of parenthood yet are quite happy to be part of conspiracy, totally underestimating the true extent and nature of parental collusion.

> The most enjoyable part of having a child was knowing that there was part of you in the total control of someone else. A feeling that you had given yourself.
> **Father of two**

WHAT TO EXPECT

Routine and rites

Trying to sort out the difference between routine and boring has taxed the male human brain for a very long time. Jobs are not as permanent and the gold watch something to dread rather than look forward to.

People change jobs more often than ever, particularly once 'boredom' creeps in. This is fine if by choice rather than being pushed but there is a fine line. Bringing home the bacon can mean putting up with the daily grind. Most people adopt patterns of behaviour transcending simply coping. Preparing for the day ahead, a crucial phone call, meeting someone, even getting washed, can carry specific actions without which there can be a feeling of incompleteness. You leave home with a vague feeling that you have forgotten something. Usually your instinct is correct and confirmed when you can't back through the door because the keys are sitting not on the top of the fridge where they should be but on the microwave for Pete's sake. Not brushing teeth before going to bed, not checking the fire guard or not locking the door all make for a night of 'oh well, I'd better get up and do it'. These

Photo: © iStockphoto.com, Nathan Gleave

routines can turn into more than just routine actions, taking on 'bad luck' status if not performed. For some people it goes even further and becomes obsessive: constantly washing hands, checking the taps, unplugging the TV and even parting hair in exactly the correct place are all potentials for an obsessive disorder.

Toddlers on the other hand adore routine as it gives safety in predictability. For dads this is important as we try very hard to avoid boredom. Getting the right balance between predictability and change is key to a toddler's grasp and confidence. Don't worry, they will soon tell you if you stray too far one way or the other. It takes a lot to bore toddlers, almost everything they come across is novel, but when it happens they will let you know.

These routines become rites when connected to a feeling of security, the use of their pet name before going off to sleep, the last hug before leaving them at the child minders or holding hands ('you're holding the wrong hand daddy'). These basic rites allow toddlers to deal with a world we have forgotten where every day presents huge challenges and novel experience. It's a bit like having a house you call home, where you know where your keys are. Well most of the time anyway. We are not alone in the animal kingdom either. From owls to octopuses routine is important for survival. So OK we don't need to worry about sabre tooth tigers so much these days but for a toddler there are very real dangers out there which rites and routine can help avoid or at least reduce the risk. Holding the 'correct' hand on a pavement makes sense if it blocks the busy road from a frail little body, open arms extended for a lift make getting across that road a great deal safer and teaches risk management. As a dad you will never be able to protect them from everything forever so these routines and rites give them a base from which to protect themselves.

So where does spontaneity come in?

Don't worry, your toddler will introduce variations on the theme if only to test its solidity. Does routine cramp original thought? Ask the artist judiciously setting up their work space before creating original and unique paintings or the writer arranging all the things they need around them before even picking up the pen. Roald Dahl worked in a shed with exactly the same things around the easy chair he sat in. Rites and routines are a platform from which toddlers can leap, knowing the support will still be there when they come back.

Structure of routine

Cramping a toddler's creative abilities is a real threat and dads deal with it in different ways and to varying intensity. In restaurants parents watch other parents inwardly tut-tutting over controlled behaviour with zombie-like kids sitting to attention while they are looking back in horror at your children tearing up the menu and eating the attractive bits. Who is right? Thankfully the range is broad and depends very much on the culture the toddler and dad find themselves. Routine does require some structure though, if only to understand how it works.

Reason

Why a particular routine and what outcome? Washing hands after the toilet is a good example, teeth brushing at night another.

Content

Effective routines don't just happen, there is usually a build up to it. A glass of milk, bed time story, favourite last TV show

all getting ready for bed. A wind down to sleep. So the routine begins and ends with an outcome.

Reinforcement

Simply running the routine reinforces its value but commenting on parts of it, highlighting what is happening also adds to its effectiveness.

Bath time

It is a sad reflection on our society that dads actually think about media hype over child abuse before bathing their toddlers. Worse still getting into the bath with them is falling out of favour in direct proportion to the number of newspaper column inches on paedophiles. Communal bathing is still common in many parts of the world and cultures. Others demand separate sex bathing but few, as far as I am aware, forbid bathing your children.

Accidents happen in baths, falls are not so bad for toddlers, although a slip-free bath mat can help when they are getting in. Scalding is much more important. Start with the cold water first and then run in the hot. Check your immersion heater will not boil the water; some are left on permanently with no effective thermostat.

Toddler baths are different from the baby version. Babies are washed, toddlers bathe. Yes, the bath is environmentally

inferior to the shower but that's because most people pull the plug after every person. Stepping into a foamy hot bath with the hint of smell from mum, dad or toddler is a special feeling never matched by any perfume.

Reason
Sharing the bathing experience is very important to toddlers. It is a time for play, reflection, education and most of all relaxation. Showers are great fun but it is difficult to think about mountains to climb, tunnels to dig, houses to build with a jet of water bashing your brain.

Content
Try to have a set time for the bath, although impromptu baths are huge fun. Some toddlers are not so keen on water no matter what it is in while others refuse to get out of the bath, swimming round like a slippery eel covered in soap, only nose and eyes out of the foam. Toys make it obvious that fun is allowed and is part of the ritual. You can expand a toddler's imagination with nothing more than the top off the shampoo bottle; think what you can do with a sponge!

Reinforcement
Bathrooms always feel colder than the bath you have just come out of so end bath time by sneaking the plug out. 'Agh! The plug has come out!' The eel slithers around in declining inches of warm water. Soon no water, just a warm towel. All part of the routine.

Saying cheerio
If you are a dad who does not work at home you will need to say bye bye on a regular basis. For some of us we leave in the morning before they are awake and return when they are asleep. Work-life balance has never been such an issue with UK men working longer hours than in any other European country. But leaving is an important ritual because it contains the element of guaranteed return.

Reason
The routine of you leaving provides a platform for a toddler to anticipate your return. Some toddlers will collapse in tears at each and every leaving but the certainty of return helps them cope.

Many languages avoid the blunt, permanent 'I'm off

Photo: © iStockphoto.com, Olga Sapegina

chum' instead choosing a softer, 'see you again soon'. This is incalculably important to toddlers. For dads being away days, weeks, months or, in terrible times, years there has to be the promise of return no matter what. Toddlers can cope with absence so long as it is not forever. Reminders of return help even though they do tug the heart strings for all concerned. Post cards have gone out of fashion which is a shame as they maintained contact in a thoughtful way. It took some effort and left a permanent reminder for the child. Phone calls are now relatively cheap and text messages even cheaper but the composed written word, read out by mum or their older brother/sister will still be there long after the phone is put down.

Content
Honesty is the best policy when leaving, saying 'won't be a tick' only to come back 8 hours later will not help the next time you go out. Giving some sort of time scale for longer times help them anticipate better. So, 'I'll be back two days before mum's birthday' or 'I will be back home when your favourite TV program is on'.

Reinforcement
At some stage you will have to leave, if they start crying you have a choice, turn round and wait or go ahead. In truth what you settle for is something in between. Constantly turning round only makes things worse in the long term, but not showing concern will equally undermine the feeling of love and being wanted. Making more of a fuss about coming through the door is better than when going out of it. Each of your returns reinforces the routine which gradually becomes more acceptable.

Beware of dads bearing gifts
Argument rages over whether dads should bring home gifts each time they are away. Travelling a great deal I used to bring home small presents each time and this generated a pattern from child to child. Very young they were not bothered about any present just the hairy man coming home, older toddlers always offered to carry my bag in and help open it, adolescents wanted to know where I'd been and why, teenagers were glued to the computer or telephone and only noticed my arrival when the dogs started barking. Now I don't bring home presents very often except from somewhere never before visited. Even this is a ritual, and shows they are not far from my mind.

PART ② Sleep

Who ever came up with the idea of 40 winks or Rapid
Eye Movement sleep? With kids you are lucky to get
a rapidly closed eye. Worse still, their bad sleep will
invariably impact on your sleep patterns as well.

Getting them into a pattern where they can control their own
sleep behaviour will pay great dividends not only for your peace
of mind but also their ability to rest as they grow into adults.
Sleeping tablets are the curse of the modern generation. If the
only way you can sleep is to take a knock-out tablet not only
creates a drug dependence it chips away at a person's ability to
look after themselves.

Yet in a way we do use soporifics, the warm glass of milk, a
story at bed time, hot water bottles. Are these the non-chemical
equivalent of sleeping tablets when it comes to depending on
them to go to sleep? Without doubt they work but then so does
Temazepam. Having their own routine for getting off to sleep will
help them in later years. Bed time stories from very rich writers
are not in short demand but tailoring stories about their security
in the face of adversity, their own ability to overcome 'bad guys',
emphasising their particular attributes towards coping will be gold
dust for later.

Going to sleep is one of the most enjoyable human
experiences. If you doubt this, watch the face of your toddler
as they slip into sleep. Being asleep is not the same as
unconsciousness or being 'knocked out'. Nature must have a
good reason for animals to spend a large part of their lives with
their eyes closed yet aware of their surroundings and toddlers
seem to need a lot of it. Sleep has many essential biological
functions and dreaming with rapid eye movement (REM) is
vital for normal development. There is no similarity to being

Photo: © iStockphoto.com, Oleg Kozlov

unconscious. When you are given a general anaesthetic for instance there is no 'middle bit' unlike with sleep where you are actually aware of the passage of time and even 'wake up', move your pillow or look at the clock yet are not aware of doing so. Toddlers are exactly the same and will wake to play with their teddy or doll mid-sleep. If you encounter them at these times they may even talk to you but are obviously still 'asleep'.

This is the wonderful thing about being asleep. You can drift in between reality and dream so easily and is much wondered by children. Adults are pretty fond of it too. On a recent survey it was found that 100% of people slept, some of them despite being asked for a glass of water on an hourly basis. Setting up a sleep pattern can help them use it in future. One of the curses of sleep is trying to get there in the first place. It's not only adults who ruminate over the past 24 hours, encouraging them to think of a strategy for sleep will help them stop the vicious circle of negative dreaming before real sleep. That they were the one who stopped the Little Pink Helicopter from coming to grief, managed to dig a tunnel to safety, alerted their mum & dad to danger on their island. Creating an atmosphere of absolute security as they slip off to sleep will pay huge dividends for future self confidence, not to mention better sleep for you as well.

These bootees are made for walkin'

When it comes to falling down a flight of concrete steps, horizontal children are less worrying than the vertical version. Turning from baby to toddler brings home the upright child with a shock.

Happily reading the newspaper about other people's disasters to find your big toe being chewed by a child you thought was asleep on the baby mat, brings home the fact that things will never be the same again, not least for your socks. Think plague of locust. Leaping lemming. Friday night tomb jumping. These children will attempt anything. The SAS motto of 'Who dares

Photo: © iStockphoto.com Yuriy Klymenko

- Can reach for an object without falling over. This comes gradually and is not helped by constantly waving a favourite toy just out of arms reach. Think a crowded bar on a very hot sunny day.
- Can turn from side to side without falling over. Some people in crowded bars are still working on this one.
- From lying down gets into the classical sitting position without any help. Finding a seat in a crowded bar is bad enough without doing it from ground level.

Toddling

The start of true walking as humans know it. Homo Neanderthals would recognise this gait if only Sapiens hadn't beat them to the post or a pulp. A sort of headlong wobbly-legged 'is this the way to the loo' sprint. Like a model aeroplane it will continue until coming against some obstruction, usually your signed photo of Tiger Woods. Clear the area and I do mean clear. TV sets are designed to take a full force head butt and toddlers tend to come off worse, shame in a way as you would have the perfect excuse not to watch *Big Brother* yet again. Lift and remove all mats, rugs, stools, toys, things to remove the stones from horses hooves, and especially dogs. As they gain confidence try them on different surfaces other than soft carpets. Kitchens tend to have

wins' is hard wired into the toddler brain. Once movement comes along there is nowhere safe for tiny toddlers or for that matter big toes, unless you constantly check their environment. Very clever doctors and child experts attempt to tie milestones by age to these developments but in truth they vary enormously between children. Rather than worrying about something over which you have little control, nature will usually sort these things out. It is better to think about the consequences of each change in ability to move under their own steam.

Stages of movement

Sitting
- When sat down they remain upright using their arms for support but will fall (usually backwards so have a pillow ready) until sitting is mastered.

Photo: © iStockphoto.com, Jaroslaw Wojcik

Photo: © iStockphoto.com, Paul Kline

more slippy floors so support will be welcome. Watch out for all the dangers of each type of room.

Walking

Hey, walking the walk and talking the talk, well almost. Some would say better than certain senior politicians. The key bit is carrying a toy *and* walking – the toddler equivalent of walking and chewing gum at the same time. More to the point they can look around as they go, always useful if you wish to be a president some day. This develops into reaching above their heads, attacking slopes up or down and getting back up when they fall over. Unfortunately the stopping bit can still be a bit problematical so reinforced glass in doors and windows, or at least covered with plastic film makes a lot of sense.

Hurtling

Now they are jumping, running, rolling, dancing climbing. Yes especially climbing. Previously you had only to worry about things at near ground level. Now they will use your book left on the floor to reach a pan handle. A cushion to get to reach a work surface. Toys suddenly become convenient ladders to mysterious but potentially deadly unlocked cupboards full of medicines cunningly disguised as sweets. The only useful advice is to get down on your knees to toddler level and see what looms above you. Lock all cupboards or take anything dangerous away and put them completely out of reach. Lock or fix all floor level windows and make sure they have safety glass fitted.

You cannot stop them from hurtling, but you can prevent them from hurting.

Hands-free toddling

The great thing about the toddler years is that dad becomes noticed. Let's be brutally honest here guys, if you suddenly found yourself in a very strange place, no idea where your next meal will come from, big fat goo-goo faces tugging at wee stubby things on the end of longer bits of useless soggy flesh and along comes a ready meal complete with 24 hour security, which would you choose:

- The nice smelly milky dangly things, or
- The Desperate Dan chin hinting of 100 proof bourbon trying to remove your outer layers of skin?

Toddlers want to know more, taste more, experience more. That's why they invariably lower their heads into the pre-digested, pasteurised, pulped textureless pap they call food. It's why they rebel at suffering the ignominy of high chairs, the toddler equivalent of the 'Comfy Chair torture'. It never ceases to amaze me how quickly the feeding tantrums disappear once out of those dreadful machines. And mate, if you are the one who frees them forever from the comfy chamber of horrors, you have made a friend for life. It's about now toddlers discover dads but beware, they want a lot more than just milk. They want *entertainment!* Some they will get from you but a great deal they will get from themselves. Allowing them to play on their own, without dictating what they should play with, is a vital part of their development. Enter toddler dad. After getting them started with bricks or an empty plastic bottle you can retire back to the other side of the room. Never underestimate how valuable this is to a toddler, and to mum and dad. Letting them use their own imagination will prevent boredom but also allow you to get on with life. So long as the room is free from potential danger you can get on with a bit of your own life, such as sorting credit card statements.

PART  Out and about

Shopping

So you thought it was bad when you took your baby to the shops, all that fuss over the trolley, trying desperately to find a nappy changing room not embedded in the women's loo. Well, brace yourself dad, 'cos not only does having a toddler mean shopping will never be the same again, you will also have to do it more often unless you go to one of those bulk purchase stores.

When it comes to entering the supermarket with a toddler you are introducing at best a semi guided missile but in all probability a rogue WMD. You have a pre-emptive chat on how reaching the checkout a reward awaits the child who fails to pull down whole rows of painstakingly set displays of tinned tomatoes (buy one get one free). This incentive lasts precisely as long as it takes for you to look sideways at the solar powered garden lights at *only £2 each!* Two things have always amazed me about toddler orifices. Despite their tiny size their bottoms can produce a motion you need to take a stick to while frantically flushing the pan, further endangering already depleted reservoirs, and their similarly small mouths can produce decibels easily rivalling a Harrier jump jet on a standing start take-off. Worse still, people take more notice of a toddler screaming.

Stores cover most areas of danger, if only to their insurance premiums, by posting large signs saying, 'Children only if accompanied by an adult'. The problem is most toddlers can't read. It's the human equivalent of road signs such as 'Horses cross here' or the famous department of education's advert addressing adult illiteracy: 'Can't Read? Don't worry, just ring this number…'. Escalators are plastered with signs which singularly fail to stop toddlers running down the up and *vice versa*. Encountering a toddler hurtling down your sedate Up escalator

> I was not too happy pushing the pram, but I got to enjoy it, honest.
> **Father of one**

> There was a time when I felt self-conscious because of 'Old World' opinions that a man with kids was strange. But my pride in my kids removed these inhibitions.
> **Divorced father**

> I had no problem with shopping except for the usual curious grabbing and eating anything within reach. I did dislike the end of the month mega shop. They and I got bored. I'm not good at debating the price of different brands of baked beans.
> **Father of three**

Photo: © iStockphoto.com, Stefan Witas

can frighten stronger men than you, dad. Stacked-up shoppers grind to a shuddering halt, much to the delight of your toddler who has just found a Big Red Button conveniently placed at toddler head height. These Big Red Buttons often carry a fine for improper use, so tutt-tutting with a 'she ain't with me mate' look on your face can help as you scuttle toddler off stage right.

Even so here are some survival tips kindly sent in by prematurely balding seasoned toddler dads.

Do you really need toddler in tow?
Decide beforehand if toddler presence is required. Can you get a babysitter or a good friend (read 'mug') to look after them while you do the business?

Pick your time
There are people who say shopping with a toddler is just great fun. Some of them write books about it. All of them spend at least part of their time staring into space weeping gently. A toddler in a bad mood is not good supermarket fun. By all means butter them up beforehand but never, ever, use the 'and we will buy some sweets' gambit. Shares in the chocolate manufacturing industry rise two percentage points every time a well-meaning but misinformed toddler owner says this.

Make a list
Dads just don't get it. There is a flow pattern to supermarkets carefully designed by market engineers to make you buy as absolutely much as possible, particularly things you don't really want or need. First aisle contains all the stuff you need to stay alive. It is usually heavy and cheap such as sacks of potatoes. As you move on the aisle contents gradually turn into impulse buying stuff which will rot in the cupboard or garage. Toddlers read a supermarket layout like a Duke of Edinburgh Award orienteer reads an Ordnance Survey map. While you flail around desperately trying to remember what you intended buying they have already homed in on the toy section, situated by sheer chance perilously close to the confectionary aisle. With a list in the correct order, lumping together all the goods in the same sections, you can at least hope for an early departure.

Tie them down
Some dads swear by those extendable leads often seen on dogs. Everything goes well until the toddler works out how to tangle the lead around an assistant's legs. At the very least this helps you find one of these rare creatures. Better still if they are small enough, use their buggy to shop with. This can double up as a shopping basket so long as you don't sling heavy bags over the handles.

Do the four minute aisle
Forget the loyalty cards/stamps/free booklets/price comparison/ items not priced/anything loose that will need weighing. Do choose a trolley which, like politicians, doesn't have a mind of its own and can be pushed in the right direction without causing too much damage to passing pedestrians doing price comparisons, weighing bananas or log jammed in the Valley of Death cunningly disguised as 'Toys n Sweets'.

Give them a job to do
By all means let them help push the trolley and yes, even use the 'mini-trolleys' supplied in many supermarkets but when you finally get to the checkout, just try to remove the bags of sweets, remote control mouse or cute n cuddly tiny teddy (no moving parts). Best of luck dad (see *Toddler tantrums* on page 47). Carrying their favourite cereal can give some distraction. Pick a BIG one with no free gift inside.

Choose the sweet-free checkout
Some enlightened stores now have checkouts without the long haul through sweets stacked at toddler eye level. The long tail back of dads with a toddler usually makes them easy to spot.

Changes on the way

Parking
One of the nightmares for a dad plus toddler is the availability of car parking spaces. Shopping means negotiating an obstacle course of speeding cars driven by frustrated drivers intent on leaving the area as soon as humanly possible, with trolley parks

requiring a mint condition pound piece the furthest distance away from the last remaining car park space. Bollards to prevent trolleys wandering but would double admirably as tank traps, and spaces so narrow that parking a car full of children means at least a re-spray after they open the doors.

Parking dedicated to parents with children, close to the entrance, such as exists for disabled drivers, makes sense and is beginning to appear. Mind you, so are 'Child on Board' signs in the back windows of thus parked cars. A lone furtive driver desperately clutching a brown paper bag of essentials for the televised World Cup match is a dead give away.

Access

While it may make sense to pack every square millimetre with sellable goods, the narrow aisle is asking for the 'Royal Mail Train Effect'. Anyone who has watched a train pick up a mail bag while on the move will recognise the analogy when taking a trolley loaded with children down a supermarket aisle. It is at this point that the analogy ends. While the mail bag invariably arrives safely on board the speeding train, the extra large bottle of tomato ketchup ends its life as a spectacular pool on the floor.

Trolleys

Supermarkets appear to believe that families consist of one child. Furthermore, the trolley is designed for a baby which can sit, unaided, in a metal framework which is ergometrically sound for folding away but has little to do with safety. A range of trolleys makes sense and is being introduced into the larger stores.

Corridor of hell, the checkout

Waiting with children at a checkout bedecked with sweets is not just a dentist's nightmare. If ever there was a more nasty side to sale promotion in a supermarket, I cannot think of it. Paradoxically, it is the single biggest reason for a parent not to go back to the same store again. Such cynical exploitation of children for profit, when the goods themselves cause harm, the manner in which they are displayed is detrimental to parental control and the pressure this exerts upon parents and children, is tawdry to say the least. When the same people who grasp for such profit deplore the breakdown in family values, it gives some insight into their perception of society. Thankfully there is a shift against such pressure selling using children, but not before time. Look out for stores which have extra staff at checkouts to help with the packing. They have been trained to 'home in' on the customers with a crying or difficult child.

Changing-rooms and toilets

Given the shift towards buying in bulk for a family, the time spent in a supermarket can be considerable. Toddlers have small bladders. For men this presents two problems: finding a toilet and finding a toilet which caters for men to look after their toddler. While there has been recent improvement, some supermarkets have changing rooms only for mothers with the helpful provision that 'staff will find room for fathers'. If ever there was a feeling of being the second class citizen, having 'staff finding room' for you must be a major contributor.

> When my three year old began to demolish the sweet display at the checkout, I turned to a woman behind me and said in a loud voice, 'madam, kindly control your child' and walked on through the checkout. It was only spoiled by (my son) shouting 'Daddy' at full volume clutching several bars of chocolate.
>
> **Father of two, still**

Eating

Just as children's bladders are small so are their stomachs. At some point toddlers will balance their growing hunger against the illegality of ripping open the nearest packet of biscuits. Given the strength of instinct for human survival, it takes little imagination to picture the scene of chaos. Having the facilities for eating is not the same as facilitating for children. Most fast-food outlets have a limited menu for children and welcome them. Some will lay on special treats for birthdays. Restaurants are not usually so keen but will still have a special children's menu, even if it does appear to add dramatically to the obesity crisis. Politely asking for a smaller sized adult meal or one between three, is usually supplied with good grace or at least a graceful grimace.

Crèche facilities

Obviously the answer to shopping with children is the same as working with children. Get someone else to look after them while you shop. You can only play on the sympathy of the next door neighbour or relative for so long. Some supermarkets have introduced crèche facilities which allows you, for a small fee, to get on with the job. Play areas are not quite the same thing but some of them are supervised. With the increased fear of abduction, it makes good sense to insist upon supervised care.

Go with the flow

Chauvinism is seen in many places. How is a father supposed to change his daughter at the swimming-pool? I once brought my four year old daughter into a men's changing room and there

Photo: © iStockphoto.com, Malte Roger

was a flurry of bare male bums going to earth. Strangely, not one single man complained but there was also not one single piece of bare flesh to be seen. This is in complete contrast to bringing in my son. There is little alternative other than to ask a passing woman to take your daughter into the changing room for you. Women have no problem bringing their young sons into a female changing room. There may be good reason for not bringing young girls into a room full of men getting changed, but I suspect it has more to do with society's expectations rather than any danger to her physical well-being or mental stability. It helps to contact the pool before arriving, they can often arrange for facilities.

On the plus side

Like most imbalances, the predicted or expected role of the mother can have certain advantages when they are reversed. Sitting on an aeroplane I had a father sitting behind with his three young children. It was not long before two men had been recruited into service as entertainers. They were serious businessmen, pinstriped suits and laptops. For the hour of flight they became surrogate fathers. Dad sat with the youngest on his knee drinking his free drinks, thoughtfully provided by a female member of the cabin staff who cooed approvingly of such male attempts at role-reversal with comments such as, 'I am most impressed'. I could not tell her that this was as much a sexist comment as that from the male television sports commentator for a women's bowls competition, who broadcast, 'There, she bowled as good as any man'.

Show a bit of leg

Sitting with four young children in a restaurant, in a holiday setting, when there *should* be a mum on hand, can raise the interest of both women and men. In such a situation, I was soon the centre of attention. From the looks of the women, children in arms, it was obvious that they were trying to work out my status. Had my wife died during the birth of our last child, her last wish that I find someone to be their new mum? Was I part of the increasing number of dads, their marriage asunder, given custody of the children because of some terrible indiscretion of my wife with a Hungarian tight-rope walker? I lived the part, wan looks of helplessness, until the women could stand it no longer and descended upon our table *en mass* with offers of help. I felt pretty good until one of the women whispered in my car, 'Marvellous, I do the same thing whenever I need a flat tyre changed'. Such was my lesson of true male emancipation. If you can't stand the heat, get out of the restaurant.

> After separation and divorce, infrequent contact has meant that the hours together carry a high premium of contact and support, sometimes too intense for both parties. There's too much I try to pack in or I expect from them.
> **Divorced father**

PART  Toddler tantrums

So you manage to get the whole way through the supermarket with little more than the Royal Mail train effect as you pass each shelf. Yes, you have twice as much in the trolley as you expected, most of it not on your carefully considered list but then a happy helper loading essentials can't be sniffed at. Slightly smug you reach the checkout still intact as a Dad In Control.

But like the Maginot Line, a manned and busy checkout is at all costs to be avoided. Not only is it a minefield of sweets set at toddler eye level, the whole area is full of people. Not just any people. These are mainly women people and they exude the 'toddler knowledge' just like when you ask a taxi driver could they please take the shortest route. Either side of narrow aisles like cattle slaughter pens there are confectionary stands with staff instructions such as, 'face this way towards the enemy'. Don't forget your toddler will have watched adverts for these tooth rotting, diabetes causing, obesity linked but wonderful tasting stuff on the TV while you thought they were very quiet in the

Photo: © iStockphoto.com, Amanda Rohde

47

living room. Within the blink of a toddler's eye you have a trolley full of 'Sour Fruits that Explode in Your Mouth'. Returning them to the stand only results in a tit for tat where you are on the losing end. Toddlers recognise an appreciative audience better than the Three Tenors. You go into stern dad mode: 'Peter, put them back please. You will be having your dinner very soon'. The checkout staff smile reassuringly. They are on an hourly rate not piecework and settle back for a rest from bashing till keys or flashing bar codes. This should be good for at least a 10 minute break from asking whether people really need a plastic bag to lift their already thrice wrapped avocado pear.

As Donald Rumsfeldt once said about another unfair confrontation, 'stuff happens'. Well toddler stuff certainly happens at checkouts and most of it appears to be your problem. Don't ever underestimate how popular you are at this moment. Rows of mums and especially dads watch with a warm glow of, 'but for the grace of…' while putting on a face of total indignation. Cheer up poor toddler dad, you have just made a lot of people very happy.

Plan A

So rewind the store 24 hour security video camera. You are approaching the sweets' aisle. Like a whirlwind of arms your toddler clears the shelves and you haven't even reached the checkout yet. This time you stop the trolley and say, 'Look Peter, if you had to choose the most glorious, wonderful most yummy bit of gear to stuff down your neck which would you go for, this aisle or wait until the *checkout*?' It never works but worth a try.

Plan B

Plan B is much more cunning. All large supermarkets must by law have a small chair available for elderly/pregnant/local advertisers/politicians/toddler parents at the checkouts. As the tantrum unfolds, and in a toddler it is truly fearsome, the

Photo: © iStockphoto.com

apparent total lack of control, head banging, fist beating, trolley kicking, shelf clearing, chest beating, hair pulling is bad enough during Prime Minister's question time but in the confined space of a supermarket your child brings back vivid images of *The Exorcist*. 'At any point now,' you think, 'he will twist his head right thought 360 degrees and with a drooling mouth ask for chocolate'. As usual in supermarkets, like trolleys without their own mind, there is not a single priest when you really need one.

Here is where toddler dad steps in. Apologise to the checkout staff, pull your trolley off to one side, and sit down on the small chair, ostensibly pulling a copy of *Women's House, Garden and Easy Divorce* magazine from the free publications rack and allow toddler tantrum to run its course. This takes great nerve. Reading about just how costly a divorce can be may change your mind about that stag trip to Prague. Having a drooling child biting your ankles doesn't help either. While people in the queue behind you are rummaging through their handbags for rabies vaccination certificates you need to stay calm and smile saying, 'it's just Peter's breakout time, he has had all his shots'.

Of course there is no guarantee this will work, not least because there is always a helpful childless woman in the queue who thinks you are Herod's answer to Bonny Baby competitions. Goo, gooing, offering whole chocolate bars while tut, tutting to you and all who can hear, and undoing your very best efforts. What you need is a plan C.

Plan C
This is cunning but requires some forethought, not generally available in great quantity for a toddler dad about to enter the world of supermarkets. As the checkout approaches along with predictable toddler tantrum, ask the checkout staff to look after your trolley loaded to creaking point while you take your toddler outside. 'Peter, we will not be going back into the supermarket unless you stop this.' A short pause, 'if you do, we can collect all the shopping and then have a treat back home'. Of all plans, this is the most-favoured by numerous mums' guides to toddler tantrums. Like many things in life they don't always translate through the gender divide. Dragging a child by one leg while

pushing a trolley full of budget beer, gadgets for taking the stones out of horses' hooves and melting plain chocolate (orange flavour) never goes down well with the NSPCC.

Plan D
Plan C also comes with no guarantee so you can always fall back on Plan D. Tell the supermarket manager you will burn down the store and film it for *Youtube* unless he gets rid of checkout aisles stuffed with carcinogenic, obesity forming, diabetes causing, teeth rotting and most importantly hideously expensive sweets. So OK, the next time you see your toddler might be during your weekly prison visit but at least there will be two inches of reinforced glass between you. More than enough for protection.

Self control
Being in control is not the same as allowing self-control. Toddlers are not daft, they know only too well when they are in control and will exploit, milk and make most use of this for their own gain. Don't knock it, this is how Homo Sapiens survived over the Homo Neanderthals sporting a much bigger brain but lacking cunning. All the sharp flints, pointy daggers and irritatingly jagged arrows were as nothing compared to good old fashioned guile. They disappeared, Sapiens Toddlers saw them off. How could

any right thinking, slightly stooped but cranium heavy humans deal with a toddler tantrum? Yet this is very much what makes us human, very young people express their demands from a very early stage enhancing their chances of survival. Well, until toddler dad counts to ten anyway. Seeing this as a positive side to child development is not easy when faced by an apparent affront to your 'authority'. But then nobody said being a dad was a rose garden. On the plus side, the way you pull through this can have enormous impact on your relationship with your child. Many children remember their tantrums with shame and would rather not be reminded. Guiding them through this difficult period helps in later life when they are faced with an obstacle they do not want to face. Rather than see this as an affront, try very hard to accept it as a challenge for a toddler dad, an opportunity to consider what works and what doesn't.

Time out
Tantrums can happen anywhere, any time and, as with the adult version, tiredness can be a factor. Setting some ground rules will help but only so long as you enforce them. Misbehaviour comes in different levels. What is considered bad by some parents is actually fun for others. For instance, stifling a child's ability to

Photo: © iStockphoto.com, Sean Locke

mimic adult behaviour might miss out on their creative talents. Singing strange tunes is not bad, it is just not quite what you expected when they are in company. There are certain things which most of us would consider unacceptable, biting people, especially their dad is not on. Getting the message across is vital and a fudged attempt makes it difficult to come back and try again.

If it is bad say so and in tones that leave no doubt in their mind that this was not on the list of OK things to get away with dad. Frightening your child is not an option, you only need a stern voice and facial expression combined with resolve to do what you tell them will most certainly happen. Saying 'you must not bite' followed by removal from the scene to some other space (but not their bedroom) will make this very clear.

Taking something they value away from them is often cited as a way to get better response but is something I have never been sure about. Try it if you think it will work but I found it only made them see you as someone to fear not love.

As with the supermarket scenario the aim is to take time out for reflection and distraction. It they are tired or unhappy over something else which happened earlier and you are not aware of, a brief time away from the confrontation will help calm nerves on both sides.

PART ② How many children?

Just exactly when do many hands making lighter work start to spoil the broth? Is two really company and three a crowd? Your long lost workmate swore he would never have another child and next time you call round there he is with wall to wall progeny. Fecundity gone mad.

Even so, big families are now rare even in developed countries where 12 children were once common. The downward pressure in these countries comes increasingly from women rather than men. In many parts of the world birth rates are so low their governments are encouraging bigger families through tax dividends. Dads must have some sort of selective amnesia or rose tinted glasses. Not long after the upheaval following child number 1 a broody look comes over their faces and before you know it the children's names book is out again.

While parents have a choice of sorts, toddlers are faced with an offer they can't refuse. Having another competitor entering the pool is not always good news. Simply telling a child that from now on there will be another brother or sister in the house is the equivalent of informing a politician that a new candidate, younger and more attractive, has set up office in their backyard. Don't expect thanks. It is an unfortunate analogy, but there is the politician's equivalent of the 'sweetener' when it comes to helping children accept the idea of a new addition to the family. To simply expect them to welcome diluted attention from the most important people in their lives, is wishful thinking. The average

> Familiarity breeds contempt – and children.
> **Mark Twain**

child can hate a newcomer to the family with a ferocity matched only by companies competing for the same contract. By showing attention to the older child, reassuring them that they are still loved and wanted just as much as ever, that their mummy and daddy brought along this new baby for them to play with, is infinitely better than ignoring their feeling of insecurity. If a small present in celebration of the event happens to be one that the older child can play with along with the new addition, so what? You, your partner, and anyone within range will be invited to join in the celebration with food, drink and happiness, why not the one who has perceives he most to lose?

Selling this to a toddler more used to undivided attention takes a bit of effort and not a little understanding of their view of life in the future. First though you had better convince yourself.

On the plus side

Your toddler might be dreaming up 10 horrible things to do to a stranger and a new baby will not help matters much by crawling

all over toddler's latest artistic creation, but unconsciously toddlers teach babies basic skills. Much of this comes from their own mistakes, catastrophes and successes. Mind you, don't be too surprised if you see baby under instruction trying to get innocent fingers into a wall mains socket. Does this mean toddler will be auditioning for a re-make of *The Omen*? Thankfully no, leading younger siblings into danger zones is normal and hopefully they grow out of it before becoming politicians. Aggressive behaviour must be accepted for what it is but not encouraged. Similarly, leaving them alone together is not a good idea.

Play is nature's way of making learning fun. Toddlers sitting baby on a potty, dragging them to the toilet to watch the amazing spectacle of dad sitting on the loo trying to read his newspaper in peace or making baby talk is actually teaching a range of skills, not least language. Baby's first words often arise from this rough and ready coaching. Praise from an elder brother or sister can also be powerful stimulation for development. Intelligence is promoted at an early age by toddlers helping baby to solve problems. Younger children also watch toddlers interact with dads to produce favourable responses, not least a hug or cuddle. Young children's lives are far from straightforward and easy, adult comparison means nothing to them. Having a brother or sister to share disappointment with can be a healthy and positive way of dealing with life's brickbats.

> Having one child makes you a parent, having two you are a referee.
> **David Frost**

Helping your toddler

Obviously a new baby will demand time, but there has to be room for toddler and it is unrealistic to expect them to 'share time'. What they crave is one to one, undivided, me-only attention. Finding this time is important, so use baby down-time (sleeping, with Mum, at their granny's, etc) for special time with toddler. Even with careful planning, toddler will want attention at times you have not written into their contract, being inflexible will not go unnoticed but then nor will an extra effort when it is obvious you are tired.

Helping look after a new baby is an old ploy and is part of the process of giving children tasks as part of the family. Many toddlers get very good at this, changing nappies, dressing a new baby and feeding, but it is easy to forget just how young they are. They still need their fun and their time with you. Sadly in many poor households around the world very young children become part of the survival battle and forfeit much of the childhood taken for granted by more well-off families. Telling your toddler this is unlikely change behaviour but a general awareness of other people's lives is important from an early age.

When to double up

As with your first child there is no perfect or ideal time to have a second, third, forth or thirteenth child. A second child is perhaps the most difficult decision for a couple and there are increasingly single children. At the end of the day, and it usually is, it will be your combined decision although I suspect some dads are faced with an offer they cannot refuse.

Next baby within 11 to 18 months
Once referred to as Irish twins until the average birth rate in Ireland dropped to turnover levels. The population of Ireland has only recently returned to that before the so-called potato famine (there was no shortage of food, a lot of it was exported to England). The small age difference has a plus and minus. Yes, you get through the difficult years quickly and can apply recent hard-earned experience to number two and they are both too young for rival sibling battles to occur. Financially it can hurt as you will need two of everything, nappies, cots, buggies, etc. If you thought you were just a tad tired first time round, you ain't seen anything yet, dad.

Next baby within 18 to 30 months
Sibling rivalry can make life a headache, especially for the new baby if your number one has anything to do with it. Watch out for that big toy hammer you bought for Christmas. Sharing out the attention can be difficult with a real danger from tantrums, hair pulling and head banging. And that's just dad. On the plus side you are less tired and need only one of everything except pairs of hands.

Next baby within 30 months to 4 years
Number one child is now quite confident and independent so baby bashing is much less likely. They also become a pair of hands but remember their young age. The fingers will be willing but the thumbs opposed.

Next baby from 4 years onward
Generally more valuable than a monkey wrench. Number one really does help out mainly in the anticipation of having a play mate. Time

Photo: © iStockphoto.com, Jaimie Duplass

is marching on however and if you started out late in life then more children equally spaced could tax your physical and mental health. At least they can go and collect your pension for you.

Shared love

No matter what your timing and number of kids at some point one child will ask which one is your favourite. Beware of this approach because what they are really asking is 'do you love me less than the other one?' Being even-handed and being *seen* to be even-handed can be very difficult, especially when you are alone to care for both of them and the new baby requires more attention. Lay on reassurance with attention by the bucket, seek their advice about what a new baby wants. They are torn between wanting to be old ('I am 2 and three quarter years old!') and being back in the place now occupied by a new baby. Simply telling them to 'love a new baby' will not always work. Similarly invoking their age as a reason for behaving well towards them can be counterproductive. 'You must protect the new baby' might just be the trigger for age regressing with a swift baby-bash from a handy plastic bottle or worse. Don't expect number one to say, 'Dad, I feel the time has come for a reassessment of our relative roles regarding the equal distribution of tangible and intangible assets'. They are much more likely to stick a lit sparkler in your ear while you are goo-gooing to number two.

Overreaction

Here comes the hypocrisy and easy to say section. Don't you just love people who say, 'Actually, I always found reading from the *Little Book of Calm* worked wonders when my child was biting through his sister's jugular vein, but then all children are different I suppose'? Nobody is as smug as a 'been there done it parent' with selective amnesia. Unfortunately it is true, remaining calm beats screaming hands down, not least because over-reacting can not only make things worse there and then, it can reinforce the kind of behaviour that provoked the reaction in the first place. To a child who is desperate for attention, any response is better than none. Making it positive and distracting will pay great dividends next time you go through the Valley of Death in the local supermarket.

PART 2

Toddlers and other animals

Tony Benn once said you can measure the civilisation of a society by the way it treats its animals. There is a deal of truth in this. Early exposure and respect for the rest of the animals sharing this planet is not a bad idea. Living on a very small farm in Ireland made this possible for us.

Fowl play

Chickens, for instance, fascinate toddlers being always just out of reach yet so tantalisingly close and colourful. More to the point they make engaging cluck-cluck noises and if you do manage to grab their tail you are left with a present of feathers to stick in daddy's ear. As toddler turned to teenager we gained three principled vegetarians. Our chickens have names, they must be fed but lay no eggs. We have octogenarian hens stumbling around on Zimmer frames asking for another biscuit.

Walking pillows

Dogs initially think toddlers are very large bones only to find out that unlike bones they will poke them in the eyes, pull their tail so hard their tonsils ache and generally make them wish they had stayed on death row in the shelter you rescued them from. There are those who would say you should never let dogs near small children. Horror stories in the press of poor kids mauled by dogs and the ever present danger of parasites particularly from dog excrement do reinforce this mantra. Yet people and dogs have been around together for a very long time and there are thankfully few bugs transferable between the two species. If you have ever watched a toddler playing with a dog it is very obvious which one is on the receiving end of punishment. No doubt toddlers enjoy it and dogs do seem to come back for more.

Regular worming is essential but so is never leaving a toddler

My husband and I are going to buy a dog or have a child. We can't decide whether to ruin our carpet or ruin our lives.

Rita Rudner

Photo: © iStockphoto.com, Cornelia Pithart

unattended with any animal. Your family friendly cuddly labrador can kill. Thousands of dogs are put down once a baby comes along and this is the ultimate extreme end of the relationship. Whatever way you feel about this, human life must always come first. For what it is worth we brought up children on a very small farm with dogs. The children were never bitten which is more than I can say for the dogs. On the other hand, I would pity any stranger threatening any of the children in front of either Finn or especially Peter's long suffering TV pillow, Megan.

Feline fiends

Cats were also around but confined outdoor. There are serious infection risks from cat excrement (Toxocara) and it is wise not only to regularly worm your cats but also remove any sand pits or soft soil play areas. They are much less tolerant of rough handling and while unlikely to attack a toddler unprovoked their teeth and claws can do terrible damage to soft skin. Despite all of this I was forever shooing cats out of the house after them being smuggled in by successive waves of toddler.

> **Facts of life children learn**
> ● Never ask a toddler to hold an egg.
> ● Cats baptise grudgingly.
> ● Don't hold a vacuum cleaner and a cat at the same time.

Tank dwellers

Terrapins have all but disappeared but goldfish are still very popular with children. There is a debate over cruelty. Swimming round and round in a glass case with no hope of release may contravene the Geneva Convention although, when applied to humans, some supposedly democratic countries seem to get along perfectly well without it. Helping to clean the tank and put in fresh water, food and things to amuse the fish helps foster responsibility towards animals. Where dogs and cats are impossible, fish in a large tank might fill the gap a little. Avoid piranha.

Caged avians

Personally, pretty birds in cages do about as much for me as battery hens. Birds were meant to fly. There is a reverse message here for toddlers: that it is OK to lock up freedom-loving creatures. Avoid vultures.

PART **2** # Losing a toddler

Thankfully, death in childhood is now very rare. As most deaths used to be caused by infection, the improvements in immunisation, nutrition and housing have all reduced the number of children dying. Even so, we continue to lose children at all ages from birth problems, illness or accidents.

Psychologists often refer to a scale which rates life events in terms of the stress it can cause. The death of a spouse or child comes at the very top. Coping with the loss of a child is one of the most difficult things to live with in fatherhood.

Losing your child through whatever cause will have differing yet similar painful effects upon you and your partner. The expression of grief can take different forms for men, given the way that we have been brought up in society. Many women will cry frequently and are able to talk openly about their feelings, while for some men there can be an inhibition over expressing their emotions.

> *When my child died, I really did not believe it. I even called the doctor a liar. My wife was crying and I told the doctor it was all his fault. It wasn't, but I had to blame someone didn't I?*
>
> **Father who lost his child she was knocked down on the road outside her home**

Photo: © iStockphoto.com, Sheryl Griffin

Photo: © iStockphoto.com, Aldo Murillo

Much of the difference in our expression of emotion can be traced to the Western stereotypical perception of what a man should do while under stress. Crying is still seen as a weakness, even by ourselves. Such a dry-eyed stoical response to grief is often reinforced by well-meaning friends who will comment upon how 'well' you are coping with your loss. Similarly they will comment on how there needs to be someone who can remain strong, to help the family through the crisis. Although this is all an attempt to help, it can put even more pressure upon the you when you have to cope not only with your grief but with this 'male' role. Few people really understand how grieving over the loss of a child can continue for a considerable time. It is not unusual for a father to weep years after their death but such is the expected role of a father and a man, it is rarely done in public.

Despite all rational thought, the death of your child can be interpreted as a failure by yourself. This misplaced 'guilt' serves only to prolong the pain and may manifest itself in changes in your personality and behaviour. Irritability, anger and short temper can be misinterpreted. Similarly, you may engross yourself in work and appear cold and uncaring. Only you, yourself, will know the internal pain. It is often not easy to share those feelings as distinct from what you do. Women, on the other hand, find intimacy in feelings easier to establish.

Photo: © iStockphoto.com, Steve Mann

DIED
21ST DEC.1977
AGED 1 HOUR.

Work

The pressure to 'be strong' extends into the workplace. You may feel obliged to return to work not only to provide for the family but also to keep your job. There may then exist an atmosphere of unreality, people are unsure of what to say to you when you do return to work, and you may be unable to perform as before. Thankfully, employers are increasingly taking on policies which are more understanding and sympathetic towards men in such circumstances. Deceptively, men will appear to have readjusted to the work routine while in actual fact are still a sea of confusion and pain.

> My mates were very sympathetic, but they couldn't really talk to me; I wanted to tell them how I felt but they just kept asking me about my wife. I felt very alone at work.
>
> **Father of child dying of leukaemia**

Home

Things are not always the same at home. With a partner in the depths of grieving, children with their own problems and yet still the everyday requirements of home life to see to. Your partner may feel an unequal burden of misery. She may have to clean the now empty bedroom, pick up the rest of the children from the same school, look after the clothes and toys belonging to the dead child. You 'get off lightly' by returning to work. Your exhaustion of dealing with work on top of your grieving makes you a poor vehicle for more pain. It can lead to distance between partners as well as unity.

> When I came home, I felt it was the same as being at work. I felt angry at my wife because she didn't have the tea made. I had worked all day while all she had to do was look after the house. Mind you, I still couldn't open the door to my child's bedroom.
>
> **Father of child dying of leukaemia**

Unemployment

Possibly worse, being at home all day may have the added feeling of hopelessness through unemployment. The anger and frustration which can build up can be manifested in many ways. Self harm or even harm towards your partner or children is a possibility. Thoughts of suicide following the death of a child, particularly when there are other pressures such as unemployment, can be common amongst men.

Photo: © iStockphoto.com, Jason Lugo

Photo: © iStockphoto.com, Sheryl Griffin

Talking

Paradoxically for men, the most valuable way of coming to terms with the loss of your child is often denied to us. Simply talking about it is important, yet for many of us we will find this difficult, even impossible; expressing grief with your children, partner, even work mates, is far better than bottling it all up inside, waiting for the pain to go away. Children can pick up the wrong messages. Not talking to them about the loss of their brother or sister can mistakenly make them think that your partner loved them more than you. It is not a great leap of the imagination for them to think this is the situation with themselves.

Just to help me sleep

People close to you will often be so shocked by the effect on you they will ask, or even demand, sedatives for you from the doctor.

Indeed, this used to be the norm and there can be no doubt that drugs will numb the pain of grief. Unfortunately, grief will not be denied and if not allowed to take its course while in the support of friends and relatives, it will resurface after the drug and the relatives have gone.

You may now find yourself 'alone' but with the heartache you should have had when help was at hand. People often talk of such an experience as 'floating above the events' only to come down with a thump later on.

Deep scars

While the wound of bereavement may heal, there is always a scar. It is there for life and well meaning comments like 'you will get over it' bear little resemblance to the truth. You do not 'get over' the death of your child, but you do come to terms with their loss. Similarly there can be no replacement, but there is solace in other children and in the love of relatives and partners. As time progresses your lost child takes on a new position within the family and home. It becomes easier to talk about them, reminisce over their behaviour and even remember their anniversaries without pushing the memory into a less painful part of the mind. Even videos, photographs and school prizes become sources of comfort instead of painful memory, but meanwhile it helps to talk and thankfully there are groups and professionals around just when you really need them.

> My child will often ask where his sister has gone. I tell him she is in Heaven. He asks me do I love her as much as him. I tell him I love him, his sister and his mum just the same.
>
> **Father of a child who died from leukaemia**

61

3

TODDLER MANUAL

PART **3** Disabilities

63

PART ③ DISABILITIES

Toddlers with special needs

> I was quite prepared to take a large cut in pay by taking a lower position in the firm. I was staggered when the personnel manager told me that he wanted me to stay on at my own post and contribute what I could until we sorted ourselves out over who would stay at home the most. I am still with the same firm.
>
> **Father of child with cerebral palsy**

Fathers often take second place in the care of children with special needs. This denies us as fathers from not only a more intimate contact with our children but also with the professional bodies which are there for support and guidance. This can affect you in many ways not least in the missed opportunity to examine your own feelings about disability.

Similarly you may not be able to meet other parents who have children with special needs, a rich source of support. Having such contact may well involve a shared fear but it also provides a common insight into the joys of parenthood.

Having a child with special needs can have an effect upon your work as an employee. Some fathers are reluctant to inform their employers that they have an increased need to be at home to look after their child and will accept or even ask for a lower paid position to allow them more time away from work.

Extra pressures

You may feel under pressure to ensure that your child has a secure future. This can make you feel that you *have* to be successful at your work or career. It can also place a perceived pressure on you to spend more time at home than you are able to provide. Having a frank discussion with your employer can often help. For many men, they are reluctant to take this step for various reasons, including a misplaced shame as if it was something to hide rather than expect help from an employer.

Relationships between parents

It is not difficult to realise that there can be stress placed upon the relationship between yourself and your partner. You can experience extreme exhaustion which has the same effect upon personalities, and the day-to-day relationship, as any other stress factor. For some fathers this can extend to their child and may even result in their rejection. It is essential in such circumstances to take some 'time out', preferably for both of you. There are groups, such as MENCAP, which will help and put you in touch with other parents who have gone through the same experience (see *Contacts* on page 183). They will give good advice such as the positive effect meeting fathers who have children with special needs. Professional help is available but requires a commitment on your part to make time to see them. Evening appointments are sometimes arranged when a father has no other time available. Fixed routines involving work are not always written in 'tablets of stone' and can be varied to suit your need to be home. This is only possible if your employer is aware that you need this consideration in the first place.

Photo: © iStockphoto.com, Luis Sierra

PART # Down's Syndrome

Physical and mental abnormalities in children are numerous, but thankfully the majority are rare. Down's Syndrome is among the commonest and while all children are unique, there are problems and joys common to looking after and bringing up children with physical or mental abnormalities. By looking at the relationship fathers have with their children with Down's, it will give some insight for fathers of children with other problems.

While nobody doubts that having a child with Down's Syndrome will place stress on a relationship, there is no evidence that there is any higher rate of divorce or separation compared with any other family. Many fathers have said that it tended to bring them closer to their partner rather than the reverse. It can be tempting to see everything through rose-tinted glasses, but happy partnerships are, perhaps not unexpectedly, least affected in a negative way. All the things which maintain a relationship are true for a family with a Down's Syndrome child. Being able to talk to your partner about your feelings is a major part of maintaining a relationship.

Time for each other

There are only 24 hours in the day, and it may often appear that there is not enough time to spare, between work, playing with the children and attending to one with special needs. Yet somewhere there has to be time for each other. Baby-sitters, relatives and respite care are all ways or reinforcing your relationship which will be the biggest single resource for your children. While all partnerships will have elements of conflict, not all will be immediately resolvable without outside help. Most parents will hesitate to seek professional help with their relationships yet would not think twice about professional help with their health. In most cases it is the unhappy relationships which occur before a separation or divorce that have the greatest effect on the development of children, rather than the separation itself. Help in the first instance can at least give guidance.

Single fathers

Professional help, along with support from relatives and friends, can often be essential for single fathers bringing up a Down's child, particularly if there are other children in the home as well. You should at least be aware of the help which is available which can be obtained from your social security office or from voluntary organisations.

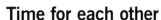

My GP is marvellous. I just mentioned that I was having a problem with space in the house and she had me in touch with the social services right away.
Single father with two children, one with special needs

Photo: © iStockphoto.com, Tomasz Markowski

4

PART **4**

Feeding and potty training

PART  **Feeding and food**

There is a world of difference between feeding and eating. One is done to you and the other is by you. Babies like feeding (think trains going into tunnels, aeroplanes landing, etc) but toddlers see it as humiliation. 'It's bad enough eating pap while you guys are chomping on pepper steak avec frites', the toddler view goes, 'without some lunatic trying to make me eat it and smile at the same time'.

Worse still, being stuck in a contraption two metres above the table only makes throwing pap at dad all the more easy. Joining the table during family meal times is not just equitable, it is fun and they pick up eating habits much quicker. There are chairs which help this but toddlers can often cope with a chair with arms plus a few hard cushions for height. So what if they make a mess of it the first few times round. Try sticking a spoon into a toddler's mouth and they will grab it off you every time, 'I can manage this thank you very much'. So OK, most of it goes in their ear but if they had something they could hold rather than glorified jelly it might go into the correct hole. Go to Greece if you want to see how toddlers are involved in the family meal, they chomp on what is on the family table not pre mashed in a liquidiser.

Nostalgia dictates that we all had amazing family meals when we were young. In hindsight nostalgia is a wonderful thing but actually my generation had a pretty miserable time of rations and table behaviour. Not being allowed to leave the table until every scrap of sprout cleared the plate, 'there are children dying in Africa for want of a sprout'. By all means I thought, pay their ticket over and give them all my sprouts, tell them to bring a big bag with them. They can start a sprout duty-free service at the airport on the way back home. Eating should be fun not a chore.

Before getting too wrapped-up in your toddler's eating habits it can help to check out your own preferences. What are your memories of meal times at home? Are you carrying over the meal mantra which you hated but because it came from your own parents' must have some value?

Photo: © iStockphoto.com, Christoph Ermel

Does your toddler scare you over food?

We are torn between kids being obese and kids being anorexic. The 'just one more sprout and you can have your bread and butter pudding' tactic tries to address both at the same time and yet answers neither. Poor eating days are invariably followed by gluttony on a scale where the jaw bones become a more pressing worry. If they are obviously healthy, happy and developing roughly along the lines you would expect then they are eating enough. Eating disorders are almost unheard of in toddlers and we do tend to be over-sensitive to 'allergies'. True food allergies tend to present much earlier in life and are more likely to be of the major classes such as lactose (cows' milk) or gluten intolerance.

Do you have particular food likes and dislikes?

It's not hard to see how a child might form a dislike of some food they are never presented with because you happen not to like it. Watch though for them holding food in their mouths without chewing or spitting it out repeatedly. Dogs putting on weight is always a good sign of food avoidance. Even so, this might be your chance to re-visit foods you wrote off years ago because your own parents refused to serve it up or forced you to eat. I can now eat and enjoy an entire plate of sprouts.

Do you talk over meals?

Across the world eating and talking, not necessarily at the same time, is part of the human experience. There is little

Photo: © iStockphoto.com, Lise Gagne

food but admittedly only with the back end of your chopsticks. Victorian dinner tables, supposedly silent except for leading comment from the father, have given way in most cultures to conversation roaming across the family table. Toddlers want to put their spoke in too, even if it is slightly less coherent and revolves around matters closer to self survival.

Are fallen spoons 'dirty'?

There are those who say we protect our children so much from natural bugs we reduce their immune capacity. Having a set of forks or spoons at hand addresses the fears of food contamination. It might be worth considering however, that they will spend a goodly part of their time sucking their thumbs after waddling across the kitchen or sitting room floor.

Do you mix fun and food?

Here is a paradox because eating is fun, talking should be fun yet we expect toddlers to take eating seriously. You can't have it both ways. Rather than have a serious eating experience make eating what it should be, fun and fulfilling. If it takes a family movie on the TV then so be it. Please save us from the regimental Sunday Dinner mentality.

Do you dress them up for biological warfare?

Wearing nappies, a huge bib and covering the area with biodegradable plastic is not normal practice for people at the dinner table although there are numerous devoted internet sites. Eating as normal from as early as possible will increase their confidence and reduce embarrassment over eating. How many eating disorders I wonder start from humiliation at an early age?

more confidence destroying than sitting at a meal table with no conversation especially if you are the one nobody is talking to. Simply sharing food is grossly undervalued.

We are so hung up on hygiene we can't even pass a spoon between family to taste yet this is part of encouraging not just experimentation but also talking about it. Consider how many TV shows there now are on food where they eat from the same plate. In many cultures it is considered an actual insult not to share food between the table members. Can you imagine a Nepalese meal without reaching across the table to taste each of the flavours? In Japan you are expected to try each others

PART  **Weight issues**

Eating ranks in the top three of favourite activities for people whatever age. Ask any TV programme producer. Toddlers are coming out of the dreadful textureless pap we force on babies for far too long. Teeth are for cutting and chewing not sucking. Part of the fun is getting their new teeth into something they can really bite.

Yet too much food is increasingly seen as dangerous to health. Obesity is the modern equivalent of TB in the early 20th century. The difference is that 'consumption' killed people slowly as they lost weight. Obesity does the opposite while achieving exactly the same result. The World Health Organisation reckons the Western world for the first time ever will have children living shorted lives on average than their parents, simply from being too heavy and taking too little exercise. We are still coming out of the WWII mentality where you ate everything on your plate. Having enough food to eat was a serious problem, now it is the reverse. Christiaan Barnard, the famous heart transplant surgeon, once let me into a secret of his longevity, 'My mother always said never eat standing up and always leave food on your plate'. Imagine how this would go down with grandparents. Mind you, he died two weeks after giving me this invaluable advice.

A great deal of what is being discussed here is about the future of your toddler. It might seem a long way away, but they will grow into adolescents, teenagers, young men and women in a blink of your eye. Making changes now will ensure their health alter on.

Eating fads are not really surprising. After feeding babies with sugar- and salt-rich baby food we expect them to wolf down

FAT FACT
Obesity in young adult life will lower your life expectancy by 5 to 20yrs.

MYTH

Obese children have a low metabolism

There is no evidence to suggest that fatter people have a low metabolism. In fact, studies have shown that the number of calories used by the body during periods of rest actually increases as children become fatter, ie, the larger you are, the more calories your body uses.

STRANGE BUT TRUE

People who consume bigger portions do not necessarily feel fuller for longer than those who consume smaller portions of the same foods.

Photo: © iStockphoto.com, Laura Eisenberg

chewy fresh foods. Toddlers trying 'real food' for the first time are not always convinced and parents will tend to take the route of least resistance. Think how hard it has been to change the school canteen menus, but obesity is not a joke. Post-war Billy Bunter has become the norm in 21st century British schools.

It is hard to escape the news about children, their diet, lack of exercise and obesity. Planning ahead will help your toddler avoid the serious consequences linked to being overweight. It is difficult to overstate just how important this is for your child and outweighs all worries over school, careers and so on. It is their health which is precious which is in danger.

Obesity in children has become the issue of the moment because we can all see that children have changed shape. National surveys show that frank clinical obesity in children has trebled in the last 20 years. But mercifully only about 1 in 20 children are obese. More worrying is that being overweight in children has doubled and now affects around 1 in 6 children. If that isn't enough cause for concern, bear in mind that most obese adults weren't overweight children – instead their obesity has crept up gradually, a symbol of their unhealthy diets and inactive lifestyles. But the problem is not so much being overweight itself – it's the tide of ill-health that follows along too.

The challenge is to help children achieve and maintain a healthy weight for life. Since weight problems tend to run in families, parents who are overweight themselves have particular responsibilities to create a healthy environment in which to bring up their children. In doing so, you can actually reap some of the benefit yourselves.

Why obesity matters

The psychological problems associated with childhood obesity are probably the most overt consequences of being overweight. Obese children can become depressed, develop a low self-esteem and lack self-confidence. In the short-term, childhood obesity can also lead to medical conditions such as high blood pressure, poor insulin sensitivity, raised blood lipids (eg, cholesterol), sleep problems and, in some cases, type-2 diabetes. The longer-term risks relate to the relationship between childhood obesity, adult obesity, habits and the health risks associated with these. Research shows that childhood obesity 'tracks' into adulthood, in other words, if your child is obese now, they have a strong chance of being obese as an adult. Obesity in adult life may increase their risk of diabetes, heart disease, infertility, respiratory and joint disorders, and even some cancers. Worse still, simply having been obese as a child can increase some of these risks, irrespective of whether you slim down as adults. Lifestyle habits also 'track' into adulthood; you know how tough it is to change your diet at 30, so get your kids off on the right track and help them to make positive changes now that will stick with them for life.

Telly tubbies

Television watching has been directly linked to the risk of childhood obesity. Studies have shown that a child who spends more than 5 hours a day watching television is 8 times more likely to become obese, compared to a child who watches fewer than 2 hours daily. The problem is made worse by poor eating habits – snacking on biscuits, crisps, etc – whilst watching telly. Worse still, the TV is full of ads for just exactly these foods.

Photo: © iStockphoto.com, Matthew Porter

Government is addressing this but the web, increasingly accessed by young children, is now also targeting them.

Toddlers are what toddlers eat

In the last 20 years we have seen portion sizes rise markedly. The problem has been worsened by 'super-sized' portions offered at favourable prices, adding financial incentives to 'Go Large'. Research has shown that people eating bigger portions are more likely to consume more calories (in part, because they do not want to waste food) but are no more likely to feel fuller for longer than someone who has eaten smaller portions of the same foods.

Couch potatoes

A shift towards sedentary activities – endless hours spent in front of the PC, playstation or telly instead of being out in the park

Photo: © iStockphoto.com, Dagmar Heymans

MYTH

Low in fat = low calories

Don't make the assumption that a low-fat food is also low in calories. For example, a chocolate bar might be 98% fat-free but yet be loaded with sugar and calories. The best way to work out the calorie content of a food is to look at the nutrition panel on the product. Information per 100g of product allows you to compare the nutritional content of one food against another.

STRANGE BUT TRUE

Kids who lie-in could be doing themselves good! Research shows that kids who sleep for longer tend to be slimmer than those that rise early. Possible explanations are that this reduces the time available to eat, that sleeping affects their hormones (and therefore their appetite) or that they are less tired during their waking hours and therefore more active than early risers.

with friends, being driven to school, etc – has contributed to the rise in childhood obesity. Declines in activity have been especially marked among teenagers.

A big fat lie

Studies have shown that the amount of fat in a toddler's diet determines how many calories they tend to eat. Contrary to what you might think, fat-rich foods don't fill them up in the same way as calories from protein or carbohydrates, so they may be more likely to overeat.

A spoonful of sugar

Sugar is everywhere, not least in processed foods often given to toddlers. Children eat more sugary foods than adults do. Children are more likely to drink sweetened, fizzy drinks, flavoured shakes or juices, snack on sweets, biscuits and cakes and have mousses, yogurts and other puddings sometimes several times a day. The biggest contributors to sugar intake in children are sweetened soft drinks. These drinks put children at an increased risk of obesity because they can be consumed in large amounts without suppressing appetite. Don't forget that these all add to their calorie intakes.

Heavy dad

Children born to obese or overweight parents are more at risk of weight gain than those born to parents of a healthy weight. A child with one obese parent is 20 to 40% more at risk of becoming obese. This figure jumps to 80% if both parents are obese – that means that 3 out of 4 children with two obese parents are at risk of becoming obese themselves! However it's not all doom and

gloom. On the positive side, any changes that you make towards lowering your own weight will benefit your kids too.

Safety fears

Fears about our children's safety have limited the opportunities for kids to get out and about and stay active. Adolescents are more likely to have their own television and a PC rather than hang out with their friends in the park or the street. As a result, children are now far less active they ever used to be. Just think about your own childhood and recall the things you used to get up to – playing kiss-chase or hop scotch, walking to your Gran's house or to school, biking to the shops to get something for mum, playing ball in the street, doing a paper round or washing cars in your street – and compare it to the lifestyle of your children today. Children are not inherently lazy – it's a trend that we've all nurtured. Personal safety is important but check that you are not being over-cautious.

How did we get this big?

Nature vs nurture

Your genes strongly influence your chances of becoming overweight or obese. Studies have shown that adopted children often take on the body shape of their biological parents, suggesting that 'nature' has an important influence. That said, becoming obese, ultimately, results from eating too much, not being sufficiently active, or both. The genetic effects may work by making some people feel hungrier, or less inclined to exercise, than friends who don't share their genetic predisposition to obesity. The big problem is that genes can be used as an excuse rather than a reason to be careful.

Does your toddler have fat genes?

Recent research has shown that a small proportion of all cases of obesity in children may be directly caused by specific genes. These genes are responsible for the body's appetite control system. Abnormalities in these genes result a voracious appetite and make it all but impossible to prevent children developing obesity In general, children may be suspected of one of these disorders if they develop severe obesity from a very early age. If your child's weight exceeds most of the lines on the growth charts before the age of 2 years, and if they are continuing to increase and they have a large appetite, your doctor may refer your child to a specialist centre for detailed genetic testing. Sometimes more than one member of the extended family will have had severe weight problems from an early age, too.

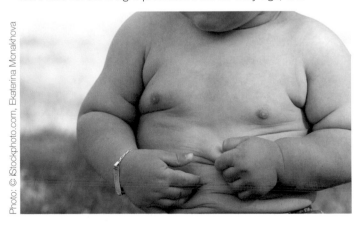

Photo: © iStockphoto.com, Ekaterina Monakhova

What are the medical causes of obesity?

A few clinical conditions are strongly associated with obesity. This includes syndromes such as Down's syndromes (Trisomy 21), Prader-Willi or Bardet-Biedl. You should discuss your child's weight with your hospital consultant and seek practical advice and support from dieticians and nurses involved in your child's care.

Some diseases or drug treatments for other conditions may be associated with sudden weight changes. This is not always fat and may often be fluid accumulation. It most cases weight may settle when the disease resolves or when treatment is completed. A small number of obese children may have a hormonal condition associated with obesity. This is usually identified and treated at an early stage. If you are worried speak to the doctor.

My toddler is the fattest in nursery school – are they obese?

Defining obesity in children is a difficult issue as children naturally change shape as they grow and develop. At certain stages of life they will tend to put on more fat and at others they lose it. Differences between children in the same peer-group may just relate to their growth patterns or timing of puberty. Nonetheless if you are concerned about your child's weight you should make some sequential measures of weight and height.

Look carefully at your family lifestyle, read the tips below with practical advice to help the whole family eat well and become more active. If you are still concerned, speak to your GP.

How quickly should my child lose weight?

Most children do not need to lose weight. Even if they are overweight or obese, many children will gradually grow into their size, providing they stop gaining any more weight now. With specialist advice from a health professional, children with a serious weight problem, especially after puberty, may be encouraged to lose weight gradually, at the rate of about half a kilo (1 to 2 lbs) per week.

What treatments exist for obese children?

Treating obesity in children is based around the same principles as adults. Changes in diet are the foundation for long-term success. The emphasis is on eating less fat and sugar, and more vegetables and fruit. Learning to choose appropriate portions of food is also critical. Obese children may find it hard to exercise because of physical difficulties or worries about teasing. Children who have been overweight from an early age may need to learn some core skills such as throwing or kicking a ball as they lose weight in order to help them start exercising.

Research in the USA suggests that group treatment programmes, especially those involving the whole family, are the most successful in changing diet and lifestyle. Gradually more clinics specialising in treatment obesity in children are being established in the UK, but are not yet available in all parts of the country. There may also be community groups, and some fitness clubs or commercial weight-loss groups may consider taking on older teenagers. Your GP or community paediatrician may be able to point you in the right direction.

In the UK drug treatments for obesity are not licensed for use in children. Surgery is a very last option and would rarely be considered until children have finished growing.

Taking action: helping them to help you help them!

One of the most effective ways of losing weight and, more importantly, keeping it off, is by making lifestyle changes that involve the whole family. Studies have shown that both children and adults are more likely to stay slim if they have the support of others around them, especially their family.

Changing eating habits and lifestyles during adolescence can be tough. It's much easier to teach your kids about the components of a healthy lifestyle before they reach their teens. If you do, the good habits are much more likely to stay with them for life and will give them with the basic tools needed to eat and exercise for long-term health. Even so, it is never too late to do something about their weight. Encourage them to adopt the action points listed below and they'll be off to a good start.

By following some very simple steps, you can help the whole family inadvertently cut down on excess calories, learn to enjoy food and take on a new and healthy lifestyle together. As a general rule we all need to eat less saturated fat, less sugar, less salt and more fruit and vegetables.

Diet

Size isn't everything
You don't need to super-size and neither do your kids. One king-sized chocolate bar provides around 20% of a 9-year old's energy needs. Choose a fun-sized bar instead – it's still a treat but at a smaller cost – just 5% of the days' calories.

Ready, Steady, Cook!
Children are more likely to enjoy their food, and try new things, if they get involved in helping to prepare it. If they reject a food the first time they try it, don't give up, tastes change fast and the more they see you having it, the greater their chances of wanting to try and like it.

Like father, like son
Set an example; a child is much more likely to eat healthy foods if they see other family members regularly enjoying them.

Get the breakfast habit
It's a fact that breakfast eaters tend to be slimmer than breakfast skippers. Eating breakfast might not turn little Johnny into Einstein, but kids who eat breakfast can concentrate for longer and perform better in short-term memory tests.

Eat meals at the table – not in front of the telly
Show your kids that you enjoy and appreciate food, rather than treating it as a pit-stop.

Snack attack
There are plenty of healthy snacks to fill everyone up between meals. Try unsalted popcorn, a slice of toast, fruit or cut up pieces of vegetables, with or without home-made dips such as salsa, guacamole, hummus or natural yogurt with garlic and herbs. Fruit smoothies made with low-fat milk or yogurt can also be a great way of getting lots of vitamins and minerals whilst filling you up, too.

Check out the lunchbox
A survey by the Food Standards Agency revealed that packed lunches were providing children with more than double the recommended lunchtime intake of saturated fat and sugar, and

Photo: © iStockphoto.com, Gary Sludden

up to half their daily salt intake. Almost half those surveyed were not getting any fresh fruit or vegetables. Crisps, biscuits and chocolate bars were common to 75% of school lunchboxes and sugary drinks found in three-quarters of cases. As a general rule, try to include the following foods in their lunchbox everyday:

- One portion of fruit and veg.
- One portion of low-fat milk, yogurt or cheese.
- One portion of meat, fish or alternatives, eg, soya, tofu, beans, etc.
- One portion of a starchy food, eg, bread, pasta, rice.

Take 5

Everyone should be aiming to have 5 portions of fruit and vegetables each day. One portion could be a glass of fresh unsweetened juice, a small salad, or a banana. You can each count a portion as the size of a handful. Keep a record and see who wins at the end of week.

Watch your drink

Talk of a drink may turn your thoughts to alcohol, but what are your children drinking? Keeping children well-hydrated is important but remember that colas, lemonades, squashes and even some juices can add to your calorie intake but provide few other nutrients, so try to limit these. The diet versions of some drinks are low in calories but may be bad for teeth. Wherever possible, encourage children to drink water. Skimmed or semi-skimmed milk is also a good alternative as it contains lots of essential nutrients but it also provides some calories, so don't go mad! As a guide, everyone should be aiming to have 8 glasses of fluid each day.

Find new ways to reward good behaviour

Keep treats as occasional indulgences not a daily bargaining tool!

Don't force your child to finish their plate if they say they are full.

Photo: © iStockphoto.com, Liza McCorkle

79

Physical Activity

Increasing activity is a great way of getting out and about whilst also burning calories, keeping fit and improving circulation. As a guide, the government recommends that we all be engage in at least 30 minutes of moderate activity for a minimum of 5 days a week. This need not be taken in one go; 3 ten-minute bouts of activity a day is just as good. Children are more likely to engage in physical activity if at least one of their parents is active so there is an added incentive for you to get active together.

Here are some simple ideas to get you and your kids up and about

● Get out the karaoke machine or buy a dance mat and have a boogie for active fun in your lounge!
● Take the kids to the park and play footie, frisbee or tag, or head out to the water park, fun park or beach.
● Encourage your children to get involved in a hobby they enjoy – they needn't be sporty ones – even painting, drama or music will keep them away from their PCs and the telly; they'll be less likely to snack, learn something new and it will keep you on your toes taking them to the classes or events.
● Walk the kids to school – they'll love you for it, and so will your partner!
● Go for a bike ride or take the kids roller-blading, skateboarding or ice-skating and show them what a big kid you really are!
● Get the kids to help you wash the car or help out in the

Photo: © iStockphoto.com

garden. Set up a rota for the housework or the washing up. Kids need to see both parents taking responsibility for household chores.

● Book an active holiday not a week lounging on the beach.
● Consider having a dog in the family – but only if you're ready to be responsible for their weight and health too.
● Have a TV-free day each week.
● Enter the family in a local fun-run and train for it together – it'll bring out everyone's competitive streak and be a real incentive to get out of the house, even if it's cold and dark!

PART  Potty training

During an interview with Jeremy Vine on BBC Radio 2 he commented on the colour photos of full nappies in the *Baby Manual*. 'That's not all, Jeremy,' I replied from a remote studio in Edinburgh, 'they are scratch and sniff as well'. Only two complaints were received.

It is very difficult to explain problems with poo unless you draw a picture. At the same time there is a relief from not having to change nappies. There are few sad sights to beat a dad wandering around with a dripping rapidly disintegrating environmentally-friendly paper disposable nappy when the sticky has failed, or tonnage exceeds terry. Seeking help from total strangers with wide staring eyes and a fistful of nappy is unlikely to elicit the appropriate response. Screaming, 'well thank you very much' and stuffing it into their handbag/notebook computer bag is unlikely to resolve the situation. What you need is a nappy-less toddler.

Children can rarely change their own nappy, and if they can they are generally too old to be wearing them in the first place. Wearing a nappy is not a pleasure, it is not only an ignominy, it can be painful and messy. Consider incontinence in later life after say, a stroke. Just because you are young doesn't mean you think they are a great idea. Getting them out of reusable towels or disposable nappies makes life easier for everyone, especially dads desperately trying to find somewhere to change them in a football ground. Parents can be over-keen to show to all and sundry how soon their ozone depleting offspring is developing, but in truth toddlers make their own decision and no amount of forcing them to sit on a Daffy Duck potty in the sitting

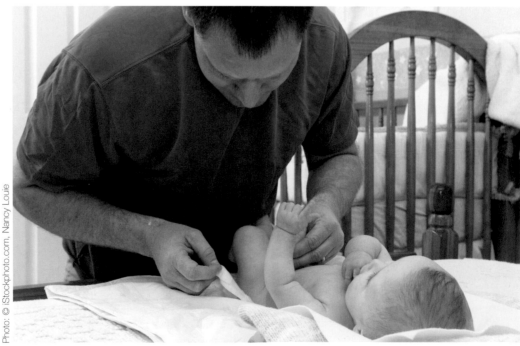

Photo: © iStockphoto.com, Nancy Louie

room during *Blue Peter* will bring self confidence any sooner.
If anything you will still be wiping up the mess by the time *Top
Gear* comes on.

Timing is all

Don't pressurise your toddler and don't be rushed yourself. There
is a clinical condition called 'Poo by Proxy'. These sad individuals
go to enormous lengths trying to get toddler out of nappies so
they can boast in front of other parents. This is also saved up for
when their grown up toddler brings home their girlfriend for the
first time. 'Potty trained by 20 months he was…'

Some pointers

You will get some idea about when they are ready from the way
they use nappies. If they stop in mid track towards their favourite
toy/dog/precipice with pursed lips followed by a satisfied smile,
you can be fairly sure without having to clean your fingernails
after poking into the nappy that they have just done the job. Now
is your chance to capture the moment. Use either a proper potty
or whisk them off to the custom-made loo adapter on your own
toilet. Don't be afraid to sit them the wrong way round so they
can see what amazing things their tiny wee bum can produce.
Let's face it, there are few things at toddler age you can take
absolute undeniable claim for and, like politicians, toddlers love
praise. Lay it on with a big spoon.

Look for signs

Toddlers' bladders empty very frequently up to around 20 or so months and obviously this is poorly controlled. Any sign of dryness during the day for a few hours, or especially waking up dry, is a good indicator of near readiness.

Poo is a different matter. While many toddlers will poo at certain times, such as in the morning or after a meal, others will constantly give you a small surprise while carrying them on your shoulders. Once they start to let you know, you will soon recognise the signs such as a vacant stare, sighing, grunting or looking for a 'secret place'. Toddlers who 'comment' on a wet or full nappy, and believe me they will let you know if only through irritation at your obvious stupidity, are particularly ready for nappylessness.

Use constant terms for urine and faeces. Expecting a 24 month old toddler to state with some authority, 'I wish to urinate and while I'm at it passing faeces sounds like a great idea' is perhaps over optimistic. Rightly or wrongly, euphemisms for bodily functions along with body parts do predominate. Allowing them to talk about these things, so vitally important to them, without embarrassment or fear will help them enormously in later life.

Toddlers pulling down their own pants, watching others using the toilet and mimicking them all bode well for a terry-free toddler in the near future.

Ready, steady, potty

I've always thought that one of life's greatest disappointments is that no one congratulates you any more for simply peeing as though you have just run the Marathon on behalf of two million starving anteaters in Borneo. (The closest you will get to it Dad, is when your prostate enlarges and you manage to get to the cinema without stopping at every pre-located loo on the way. Always remember the definition of male middle age: It's when your prostate is bigger than your brain.)

Encouragement and praise are both vital. Talk them through it, explain what the noises are, not to stick their fingers in it, not to

Photo: © iStockphoto.com, Don Bayley

stick their fingers in your nose, etc. Try using their favourite doll, teddy, alligator to show what happens. Your facial expressions along with Mr Bean like noises do the trick better than asking them to look it up on *Google*, believe me. Far less adverts, too.

Getting them onto the house toilet changes your life, you can use an adapter which prevents toddler disappearing bum first and gives them confidence when the toilet is flushed. Most toddlers are fascinated by what comes out of their bodies so give them a chance to study it, it is your chance as well to make sure things are as they should be. Use positive noises and words rather than expressing how horrible poo is. Most toddlers have an innocent affection for what they produce. Flushing the toilet should be the final congratulation. 'Whoosh! Another half ton of manure for the tomatoes. Well done Bertie'.

The basic genetic difference between boy and girl toddlers is direction. Girls wee downwards; boys wee upwards. This is important for nappies but vital for potties and toilets. Encouraging them to push their penis down as they wee will pay huge dividends when they hit middle age where sitting down seems to make such good sense. You can buy deflectors but self control is better.

Training pants are not pants

As with nappies there is a debate over the environmental impact of disposable training pants over the cotton versions. Their big advantage, easy disposal, might be an illusion as it prevents to some extent the toddler's awareness of a full or wet pair of pants, an important part of training. Bare bums are still important even when out of nappies. Yes, there will be the occasional accident although they often help the whole training process so long as you don't make a fuss over it, but a dry bum exposed to the air will avoid infection and irritation. Whatever you choose, eventually your toddler will be able to wear cotton pants and remain dry and clean.

Photo: © iStockphoto.com, Monica Adamczyk

Happy hygiene

So OK, we are perhaps obsessed with cleanliness. Television adverts and programs don't help either. Increasing allergic reactions are put down by some researchers to lack of exposure at an early age to good old fashioned muck. Even so…

- Get boys to squeeze their foreskin (if present) to get rid of the last drops.
- Girls should wipe their bottom from front to back to prevent infection from the anus to the vagina.
- Both should avoid over zealous wiping, not just to avoid pain but also subsequent infection.
- Get them started in the practise of washing hands after going to the toilet early but beware Dad, they will also watch what you do after having a pee as well.
- Wash hands together. It's fun, especially with slippy soap. Fingers hidden under soap suds are magical, driving their imagination wild.

Cheer up Dad, soon you can stop sniffing your finger nails and eat your chicken drumstick without squinting.

Photo: © iStockphoto.com, Monica Adamczyk

5

PART **5** TODDLER MANUAL
Child care

In someone else's arms

Let's face it, much as it hurts, at some point someone else will look after your toddler. Generally speaking, nobody is enraptured over this fact but there will come times when, even with a partner, a childminder will be required. This might be the first time your child has been in the care of another person so be prepared for some fireworks although there are ways of defusing the really spectacular displays. It's not all bad news either, being away from mum and dad for a short time with the cast iron guarantee of return prepares them for later life, not least going to nursery, pre-school or school itself.

Choices

There are many ways of having your toddler cared for in your absence but a great deal depends on a number of factors:

Age

The toddler years span a vast range of experience, knowledge, ability and cunning. Younger children tend to be deeply upset but then find the childcare interestingly novel so long as it is not too prolonged and they are in the right hands. After an initial withdrawal, older toddlers can often relish the challenge a new person can give. Your choice of childminder is important not least because they will be a key step in your toddler reacting and responding to people in authority. Too harsh and their natural

Photo: © iStockphoto.com

testing, a part of setting out their stall, will be crushed. Too soft and they will learn a whole lot of new tricks to make future teachers' lives, not to mention your own, a challenge which could be done without.

Personality

When it comes to personality, no two children, even within the same family, are the same. Getting the right person who will bring out the best in your child, matching their quiet or boisterous nature is not always successful first time round and if your child seems unhappy then you should seriously think of not waiting too long before making the change. It is amazing just how differently childminders view toe curling behaviour or indifference.

Finance

Worries over filthy lucre are never far away when you are bringing up children. Fear not dad, by the time they are admiring a second-hand car or contemplating university you will look back on this time as the bonanza times. You don't need to win the lottery but it would help. Childminders don't come cheap, especially if they have a string of qualifications after their name. Gone are the days of slipping them a few quid to nip down to the cinema with plenty left over for a bag of chips on the way home. We are talking serious money here and a significant amount of your daily bread will be eaten before you get anywhere near banking your pay cheque. Before you tie the knot with your beloved and certainly before you stop the contraception check out her family. If she has two full sets of grandparents, parents, younger siblings or a gullible best friend you can plan for at least two toddlers without taking out a second mortgage. Relatives are the great unpaid workers in families.

Duration

The amount of time and how often it will happen is crucial to your choice of childminder. 'Latch Key' children are becoming an increasing phenomenon these days where both parents go out to work and toddlers shuffle 'tween relatives and childminders. It's not unusual for dads to have more than one job, putting even greater strain on childcare. In an ideal world there would be no need for 'outside' childcare and some countries recognise the value of parental care giving appropriate paternal as well as maternal state support.

Options for care

The biggest danger is opting for the least of a bad job. It's worth remembering that this will be the first time your toddler is completely in the hands of another person and that they might well be a total stranger to all concerned. On the plus side it will be for a limited duration so going for your reachable gold standard makes sense even if the woman with a haunting single malt perfume did come highly recommended by a friend of a friend you met in a pub only charges £2.55p per hour (except Friday nights).

Photo: © iStockphoto.com

Home, not alone

Why pay some company's rates bill or help to heat your mother's house when you can bring a childminder to your own home? It makes sense financially, at worse you might have to pay travel costs (tip: always ask do they enjoy cycling). A poor choice may also lead to the unexplained disappearance of your favourite gold cuff links (probably lost them at that company bash you brought in a childminder for). Your toddler by definition will 'feel at home' with all their favourite toys at hand and most of all that delicious knowledge of how to change TV channels with the remote while the childminder is watching *News 24* oblivious of *Teletubbies*.

Disadvantages

Perhaps the biggest loss is social interaction. Most minders will go for the route of least resistance and dealing with a gang of other children as well as their own charge rates low on the Richter scale of job satisfaction. In terms of your own job you face a crisis if they ring in sick and you are left literally holding the baby. Potentially worse is the effect the relationship within your home may have on your own attempts to woo their love and affection. Being there for a tiny fraction of their waking hours never goes down well, especially in the story-telling department.

Day care

This is the middle ground between home and institutionalised care with a carer looking after children in her (or his) own home or base. This does give the feeling of intimacy of home life and with other children to mingle with. Yes there may be less chance of infection from large groups of children but early exposure to, for instance, chicken pox might not be such a bad idea. Many of the allergy syndromes are put down by some people to a lack of exposure at an early age, denying their immune system's ability to recognise non-threatening allergens. They also get to meet other children from other backgrounds. This can be a low-cost high-gain alternative leaving you with a relatively low risk to your outside work. It can also be flexible to your advantage, extra money can mean extra care time. But STOP dad, think relationship not convenience.

Disadvantages

Unless you have the time to really check out their health and safety commitments you might find they aren't what you would expect. This is particularly a problem if they are unregistered. If she or he becomes ill themselves they may need to close down the care centre leaving you with the need to find an alternative, often at short notice.

Day centre care

Childcare has become big business. Lack of full government financial support has not stopped the growth in demand. Children from a range of ages are cared for by qualified staff in a central location. This can vary enormously from gifted amateurs to well-qualified staff, often a mixture of the two. There are huge advantages not least the flexible hours often on offer, a programme suited to your toddler's needs, all the equipment to foster better development and above all meeting other children of the same age. Replacements for sick staff are usually guaranteed and it becomes their problem not yours.

Disadvantages

Serious dosh time. The insurance cost alone will make it impossible to operate any kind of childcare unless they can offload it onto the parents. This means you. For every pound you make you are using a goodly percentage on childcare. Most of this is a good investment but you do need to check it out, just like you would want to know what is under the bonnet of the second-hand car you're about to buy.

Nursery school (pre-school)

Think school but more nappies. Pre-school is popular with governments so long as parents pay up front but the evidence for better academic performance is very thin on the ground. Better to think of it as a mixture of childminding and formal education rather than an open ticket to a Nobel Peace Prize. They tend to follow the state school calendar so it is easy to forecast when to block out the holiday periods; similarly, by definition they interface with their upper school partners. Most schools have a 'reception' phase so it is argued that children who attend pre-school are simply brought back to base line. Even so they will be exposed to social mores and more childhood infections. You on the other hand will be exposed to significantly mores on your bank balance; pre-school, unless state provided, does not come cheap.

While there is no shortage of choice you will need to make some hard-headed decisions when choosing a nursery school.

Age

Most nursery schools accept children from the ages of three to five, though some cater for slightly younger children, too.

What's the difference?

Yes, it does matter. There are nursery schools and nursery classes. Nursery schools are independent of schools for older children, whereas nursery classes are attached to primary schools, which means the head teacher of the nursery runs the main school too.

Money can also come into the equation. There are state-run as well as private nursery schools and classes. State-run schools

and classes are free: all children under five in England are entitled to at least 12.5 hours of free education per week for 38 weeks a year, though you normally have to pay for meals and trips.

Private nursery schools can charge £1,000 and more a term in fees (though some private schools offer free part-time early education places for eligible three and four-year-olds).

Depending on where you live, you may also have a community pre-school nearby. Community pre-schools, often run by parents, are organised on a not-for-profit basis but normally charge a fee of up to £5 a session (again, they may offer some free part-time places).

Fact-finding made easy

Your local education authority has information on state nursery school. Its worth checking out locally rather than nationally as each area is different in the way it offers services.

Perhaps the best way is to ask other parents in your area. A great deal of useless pain can be avoided though asking those who have suffered before you sign up.

In addition to your local authority, you can contact your local Children's Information Service (CIS) for more details about pre-schools near where you live (see *Contacts* on page 183).

All nursery schools are the same?

Sadly no. Always visit the schools in your area before choosing. Talk to the head teacher and have a good look around, taking notice of how happy, safe and calm the children seem. First impressions can count but there are some things to watch out for:

● What was the welcome like?
● Are the staff moody, over-worked, irritable or easy going?

- Do the kids talk to the staff by name?
- Are there junk food machines?
- What's on the menu, turkey deep fried bits?
- Are the toys time wasters or mind expanders?
- Do the staff join in with the games?
- Is anyone smoking even in the toilets?
- Do the rooms look bright and cheerful, and is there plenty of space?
- Is the school clean and well-kept, are the bathrooms clean and hygienic and does the outside play area look safe and secure with no access to the road?
- How experienced are the staff and what are their qualifications?
- Can you get there in a hurry?
- How limited are the places?

More to think about

You probably don't have the time to check out every single nursery in your area but you can narrow your choice down to three schools and check their Ofsted inspection reports (see *Contacts* on page 183).

If you're considering a state-run nursery school or class, apply to your local authority (many have a website where you can apply online).

If your child does not qualify for any schools you have ranked on your nursery application form, you'll be offered the nearest nursery to your home address with an available place, unless your child is in care, if they have special educational, any medical or social needs, or unless they have an older sibling already at a school.

You can of course consider a place at a private nursery school and apply to the school direct.

PART  Preparing for Big School

One of life's brutal lessons is that there is always someone bigger, brighter and bolder than you. Just when you are top of the nursery tree you get shipped off to Big School: The Infants.

Nothing is as daunting for a person as first going to infants/primary school. For starters the children all appear enormous. You thought as a toddler your sister was big but look at these guys! They can eat a small child a day for breakfast and still not feature in the National Obesity League Tables. And look at the teachers, they are straight out of Harry Potter. And the desks, they are made for giants but look at where you eat, there are hundreds of huge people in rows like a Dunkirk beach on a bad day. And the playground like some sort of concrete demented hell with huge people dashing around bashing into tiny people all huddling together like very small Emperor penguins watching out for killer whales.

The first day at school

The first day at school can be tough for both children and parents. But with a little preparation, it'll be easier for both of you to cope.

Before your child's first day at school, it helps if they have the practical skills their school will expect, such as being able to sit down and listen even if for only a limited period. Being perfectly toilet trained is not always a requirement, but helps.

Give your toddler an insight by walking them past the school,

Photo: © iStockphoto.com, Liza McCorkle

Photo: © iStockphoto.com

especially the playground. It obviously helps if you already have another child who you can involve in the conversation. Unfortunately they can often do the toddler equivalent of the 'worst job I ever had' routine, accompanied by wide eyes and even wider sphincters. There are picture books about starting school, but being there with them makes all the difference.

Whatever your child's reaction to school, never underestimate the level of professionalism and experience of the teachers. They have seen it, done it and, in the vast majority of cases, would not be doing the job these days if they weren't more than just good at it. Rather than the Wham Bam approach, most schools now bring toddlers in on a gradually-increasing basis. This can be tough on your own schedule but it is worth bearing in mind that one of the most enduring memories of school is that first very early contact and it can flavour development for a very long time.

Don't expect instant adoration of their teacher although it is amazingly common and can cause more than just a twitch of jealously. Some toddlers refuse to go back and it is usually separation or unfamiliarity that triggers it. Don't force them, take the teacher's advice, and be around if they think it will help.

Also, don't expect a straight answer to 'how did your day go?' Ask leading questions such as: 'Who did you play with? Who did you eat lunch with? What's the playground like?'

The teacher is your friend, not to mention your toddler's best mate. They are highly-trained but also tend to gravitate towards primary schools though empathy (both men and women). There is art as well science going on here. It's essential to make the teacher your first port of call if you think something is going wrong. Criticising them on the basis of what your toddler has said is unfair, give them open ground to help you. Be prepared to hear what you maybe did not expect. Children are very good at manipulating your emotions and have been at it all their short lives. This is your toddler's first chance to be on the ladder to independence and they are on the first rung. Don't let them slip.

For more information on coping with first day nerves see Directgov's *Preparing For The First Day Of Primary School* (see *Contacts* on page 183).

PART **6** **Work-family balance**

PART  Flexible working

You may be among the increasing number of fathers who now stays at home while your partner goes out to work. Over the past decade there has been an increasing emphasis on part-time work. Women have been at the forefront of this change but men also are seeking such employment.

> When my wife went part-time at her job I felt annoyed. She spent time at home and looked after the kids. With all the redundancies at our plant I applied for part-time rather than lose my job completely. It was the best thing I ever did. Now I actually get to see the kids before they go to bed.
>
> **Father of three**

In general practice, for instance, once considered a male domain with full-time work the norm, there has been a four-fold increase in the number of part-time posts since 1990. This increase is not confined to women. Men are looking for more than just a job as the centre of their lives. With the shift in employment patterns, it is becoming clear that there will be a corresponding change in the way we look after our children. While it may be reasonable to state that whoever happens to be at home is the 'carer' this dubious state of affairs is already under pressure and is doubly so when both parents want to pursue careers and go out to work. By making it easier for parents to look after their children and still pursue their careers, it can prevent the loss of highly-trained personnel while at the same time improving life for the family. Both of these facets make economic sense.

It can be argued that the smallest unit of democracy in society is the family unit. From this unit of democracy we need to impress upon government that as fathers we should have the right to share in the upbringing of our children rather than simply being a provider.

How do we supply life skills to our children which also includes parenting skills for life as adults with their own children? It is remarkable that while we constrain children's education through the National Curriculum, there is little effort made to prepare them for their greatest challenge, that of being a parent themselves. It will take a positive attitude from the government and educational bodies to help children understand the changing role of fathers and the need for flexibility in the way we employ both men and women to allow them contact with their children.

For parents to be able to look after their children to the highest level, there needs to be a change in the way governments and employers approach the interaction between work and family life. The expectations of parents are probably too great given the unfriendly family policies which exist in the UK at present.

> When I asked my boss could I have a few weeks off because my son was coming out of hospital he asked 'was I still married?' I wanted to be there, as well as my wife, but jobs are hard to find.
>
> **Father of child with leukaemia**

> Part of the reason why we split up was over money. I felt that I was just a cash dispenser, a hole in the wall. I wanted to get closer to my kids but I had to work to get money to keep them safe. Now I still supply the money and see even less of them than I did before.
>
> **Divorced father of five children**

PART  Changing roles

Not only are more women taking up employment, but they are also increasingly returning to work after having had a child. Where there is little difference in pay between the father and mother, the decision on who should remain at home to look after the children is no longer automatic.

Society still has a jaundiced view of men remaining at home while the woman goes out to work, but it is changing under the pressure of events.

The changing roles of sexes has shown that there are increasing levels and examples of role discrimination. A great deal of this comes from the way money comes into the family home. We are still in the position of women looking after children and men going out to work, and when this alters there is little to support men in their role as carers of children.

> Money ruled our family. I couldn't take time off because I had to pay for the freezer, the television and the car. When my partner got a job I felt threatened at first; I was the one who paid for everything. It took a bit of getting used to.
>
> **Father with two children**

Photo: © Stockphoto.com, Leeh Marshall

There is still a resistance towards discussion of these issues at work. Many men have to sacrifice their family life in order to be able to pursue careers; the sacrifice, however, works both ways, and families can be effectively 'fatherless' because of the pressure of work. This has been amplified by the current obsession with 'efficiency' where one person will often do the job once performed by two or more. Very little attention has been directed towards the effects these changes have upon individuals, their families and the structure of society in general.

It is becoming increasingly clear that we need to make some decisions about the emphasis we put on work compared to family and play. The overtime which will provide for the CD player or promotion which brings with it responsibility but more time away from home, will all have to be considered in the light of being a real father, rather than simply fathering children. This could never be more true than for the early developing years of our children.

When there is a reduction of office staff to a point where there is little, if any, overlap of responsibility, the pressures increase on individuals not to take time away from work for any reason. It can become so intense that men will take work home with them, further compounding their already reduced contact with their children. Unless work practices include an element of 'slack', this pressure will have effects not only upon the family of the individual but also upon their personal capacity to function. Many employers now recognise the value of allowing employees to get on with their work as freely as possible from stress generated from whatever direction, particularly the home environment.

Photo: © Stockphoto.com, René Jansa

PART  Family-friendly policies

Some employers have taken the lead and are introducing employment practices which allow men to maintain their contact with their families. This is not simply altruism, increasingly employers are recognising the value of policies which are friendly towards the family. Not only do they retain highly-experienced staff but also improve job satisfaction and therefore the quality of work produced by both men and women.

One bank, for instance, has established nurseries to allow both fathers and mothers to return to work. They have extended this to holiday play schemes and have maternity leave for longer than the legal minimum required.

Men are particularly prone to becoming 'stale' in their attitudes when they have been pursuing the same work pattern for a number of years. To refresh and introduce new ideas while at the same time allowing men to take more responsibility at home, the bank is encouraging 'career breaks'. This has led to more men and women looking for job sharing – perhaps the pattern for the future.

Benefits

1 Improved morale increases motivation.
2 Reduces absenteeism.
3 Retention of skilled staff.

It is gradually dawning on employers that for every £1 they invest in family-friendly policies they derive much more in improved work from both men and women.

> I used to work 56 hours and bring home the accounts. The kids were in bed when I got home and were still there when I went out in the morning. I may as well have been on my own. Now I share my job with a woman who also works part-time. I write, play the guitar, play with the kids. We sold the second car and the caravan. The kids have less money and more dad. Tough, I tell them as I fight them all on the bed.
>
> **Father of four children**

Photo: © iStockphoto.com, Zsolt Nyulaski

PART 6 — WORK-FAMLY BALANCE

Divorced and single parents

You cannot help but be aware of the changes which are taking place in society with respect to long-term relationships and marriages. Children are often involved in the breaking-up process.

While it has been shown that children are better off once their parents have split up if there is violence or extreme levels of stress involved, it would obviously be better if the family unit did not need to divide in the first place. The trick is to keep families together from desire rather than coercion.

> There was a wall between us. I could almost feel it. We used to use the children to hurt each other, like swords. That was the worst bit. Now I don't even ask about my former wife's partner when the kids come round. I wish I had them instead of her, though.
>
> **Divorced father, paying maintenance**

PART  Recent changes within the home

Not only have there been dramatic changes in employment patterns which have had their effect upon the family, there have also been changes taking place within the family home itself.

Life expectancy

Both men and women are, on average, living longer. Traditionally older relatives were looked after within the family home and this provided contact between the older and younger generations.

Women were always seen as the obvious carers but this is changing and men are finding themselves as both fathers and carers within the home. Little provision is made for women within the workplace to be able to perform these caring responsibilities and even less for men. This places greater strain upon fathers and their relationship with their children.

> The first we knew of her accident was when the social services rang us to tell us we had to pick her up from the hospital. I hadn't seen her for 26 years, and suddenly she lived with us. Two of the children had to move into our bedroom. I didn't really mind, but we had different ideas on how we were going to live in the future. That's all changed now.
>
> **Father of four who looks after his 82 years old aunt with a fractured hip**

Photo: © iStockphoto.com

PART  **Travel and holidays**

PART  Holiday survival guide

If you are reading this book for the first time on a plane, boat, train, car or white water canoe it is too late. Place the book between your knees and take up the brace position. If however you are sitting at home contemplating a family holiday, congratulations. Unlike Captain Oates you may be away for some time but actually return. This part of the book is for parents who want to remain parents even after their annual family holidays.

Family holidays are scary things

No matter how bad it gets, be reassured that family holidays must come to an end and that soon you will be safely back at work. While there is room for optimism and some parents report spontaneous smiling, survival is the main thing. Don't knock it. Simply being able to look your mates right in the eye and say, 'We have just returned from our annual holidays' without shaking, drooling from the side of your mouth and losing all bladder control is a real achievement. You need a level of preparation not dissimilar to that required for the D-Day landings along with courage, determination and sea-sick pills. Nothing else will guarantee parental sanity and with a bit of luck you might break even and actually enjoy yourself. No honestly, it is

possible. The author sacrificed his own mind and physical health undergoing hands-on experience with a total of four children taken to places all over the world so that you, the fortunate reader, have an evidence-based route map to mental stability and you don't even need to read it upside down.

While you might not be able to actually relax, you can face any journey by any form of transport in any country for any kind of holiday your children desire, although a trip to Disneyland may require reading this section twice. Without doubt the challenges are not equal nor are the rewards the same but at the end of the day, and it invariably is, you will not need electro-convulsive treatment on your return home, or even while you are away.

Anyone who tells you that travelling 600 miles non-stop with a pregnant partner and three young children in an aging Peugeot 205 is something to look forward to is either a pathological liar or has spent too much time in Barcelona. Similarly, camping is not for the faint hearted, especially if you are short on memory and big on needing to get up in the middle of the night. Saucepans do admittedly offer a tempting alternative to barefoot treks *sans luminaire* seeking the distant French 'stand up' toilet block. Breakfast, however, may never taste quite the same again.

So why do we subject ourselves to this annual flagellation? Is it because we did something really terrible in a former life? Many parents now go for *two* family holidays each year and they can't all have formerly been Vlad the Impaler or Attila the Hun. No, the reason we do this to ourselves rather than simply push safety pins through soft protruding body parts is because our children tell us to.

'My best mate Billy went to an activity camp in the Australian outback with his mum and dad. There were *real crocodiles* to play with! Can we go mum?'. Any response along the lines of 'You will just have to ask your father' is weak, defeatist and I must say, coming from a dad, utterly indefensible treachery.

How to be mentally prepared

Arriving late at the airport check-in after fighting city traffic, desperately seeking car-parks closer to Budapest than the terminal and queuing for two hours only to be told the passports are out of date is now grounds for divorce. Not specifically for neglecting to check all travel documents six months ago when you booked the holiday but rather for the physical assault by your wife using a small child as a club.

It's not just documentation either, you need to prepare your mind. For 'family holiday' substitute 'hostage taking situation'. While these obsessed and single minded captors might not necessarily resemble the classical terrorists as we know them, your children can wreak just as much brain homogenising damage as any guys wearing balaclavas well trained in pulling out toe nails. In fact, the British soldiers are encouraged to take numerous family holidays as training for any potential hi-jack. If you can survive a fortnight in the Algarve with four children then seven years solitary incarceration in an Afghanistan cave is easy-peesy. One lance corporal reportedly refused to be liberated because it was the middle of June and he knew what was waiting for him back home.

List of things to bring
Do not leave home without these:
- Paperwork such as holiday insurance.
- EHIC form if in Europe.
- Blood group info in case of accidents.
- Tickets.
- Passports.
- Car hire info.
- Maps.
- Accommodation info.
- Phrasebook.
- First aid kit.
- Medication (leave in its box, and include a prescription).

PART

Carrying babies and toddlers

Once upon a time you carried a baby or toddler in your arms while in the car, not least because there was no choice. Unfortunately we learn the hard way and now there are specialised safety systems to protect your child. Similarly, babies were left to wander around homes with stairs mountaineers would look twice at.

Buggies

These devices grew out of a need for lighter more versatile transport than the pram. They are generally a lightweight, quick to fold, push-and-go-anywhere vehicle designed as much for ease of use as storage. They can collapse into a long-thin shape (umbrella folding), or may fold flat. Frankly, there is little other option for a dad who is going to use public transport or travel overseas. Airlines generally welcome them but only in the hold. Car use is also made easier, especially when compared with trying to get a rigid pushchair into the boot, unless you own a very large 4x4.

H34151

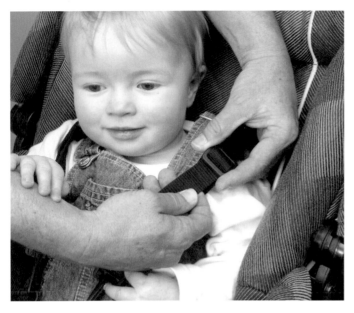

There is a huge variety of options for buggies. Look out for:
● Buggies which fully recline as they are suitable from birth. The most basic models do not recline and are only suitable from age three to six months.
● Ease of opening and collapse.
● Lightweight.
● Freestanding and stable when collapsed. (Some will infuriatingly run away on two wheels.)
● Washable covers.
● Five-point harness, easily adjusted.
● Guarantee.
● On/off swivel on the front wheels. Vital for supermarkets/long walks.
● Blow-up tyres give a more comfortable ride than solid ones. They also make for easier pushing, but only if you keep them blown up.

Double pushchairs

If you need one of these, congratulations, you have just entered the equivalent of the two car family. There are variations on the theme of getting two children into essentially one machine:
● Facing each other.
● In-line with both facing front/rear.
● Side-by-side with two pushchairs joined together.
● Side-by-side with one very wide pushchair for two.

Twins will grow at the same rate, so the side-by-side options or in-line work equally well. Children of different ages can be more tricky and tend to need more cumbersome machines, but generally side-by-side models may be too wide to fit through shop doors. Face to face, in-line models are narrower and therefore easier to take into shops, but they may be quickly outgrown if there's not enough leg room.

Car seats

Car seats must always be used and be certified to the latest European standard (UN ECE R44.03) or better, although a child is still far safer in any car seat than in no car seat at all. Beware second-hand car seats though unless you are perfectly sure of their history - for instance if they are from another family member.

There are some exceptions to using a car seat: in the rear of a taxi or in an emergency vehicle.

Some things are more than simply desirable:

- The seat must be the correct size for your child.
- The seat must surround the child's head.
- The seat must fit into your car correctly and into any other car you are likely to use it in. It is worth asking the retailer to demonstrate how the seat fits and to check that it is suitable for your vehicle(s).
- Securing clamps must stay in place if the seat is to stay safe. Get advice from a qualified mechanic if necessary.
- The shoulder harness must allow for growth by maintaining a correct fit over the shoulders.

- Padded harnesses prevent chest damage on impact.
- Unless impossible to fit you should always favour rearward-facing seats, which generally offer better protection than forward-facing models, particularly in front impact accidents.
- Never use a child seat in the front of a car equipped with airbags, unless the passenger airbag can be disabled. See your car's handbook.

Travel cot

Most hotels will supply cots. Even camp sites, particularly those on the Continent, have caught on to the needs of young families. Travel cots are invaluable, however, for the occasional trip to relatives or in a caravan. Choice is generally dictated by how you intend to travel or stay.

Travel cots are the work horses and have been around for ages. Unfortunately they sometimes tend to look that way as well and can be very heavy and difficult to erect. They usually consist of a sturdy fabric cot on a frame, which folds down into an oblong shape and often packs away into a zip-up travel bag with carry handles.

Check out:
- Does the mattress come with the cot?
- Is it good quality with a cover that is washable/wipeable?
- Is one side made from mesh with a roll-down blind to make the cot darker for sleep?
- Can you easily erect it and fold it up again? Asking the retailer to show you how it works is worth hours reading the instructions (pride permitting).
- Does it double up as a playpen?

H34177

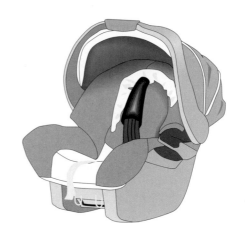

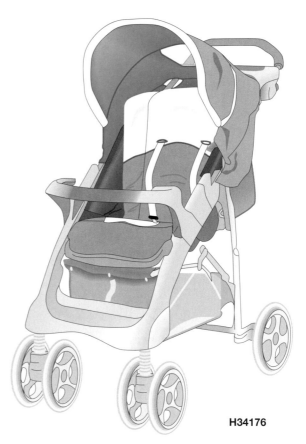

H34176

Travel systems

These sophisticated bits of gear allow you to attach an infant carrier car seat onto a pushchair chassis. Ideal for use if your lifestyle has you frequently in and out of cars. They also enable you to take a sleeping infant from the car to the house without waking up (if you're lucky). They vary greatly in cost and ease of use so check out:

● Does the carrier car seat fit securely in your car?
● Can you get the fitting done by the retailer?
● How easy is the pushchair to erect and collapse?

● Are the attachments to the car simple and secure without requiring too many fixing attachments?
● What is the weight and size of the whole machine when erect/ collapsed?
● Does it come with a range of accessories? (rain cover, toe cosy...)
These systems are designed exclusively for rear facing positions in the car and must NEVER be used with an operative airbag.

Very young children need to lie flat regularly. Don't leave them to sleep in an infant carrier car seat for prolonged periods.

PART  **Travel**

Cars

It was once compulsory for a man carrying a red flag to walk in front of the newly invented car. This was to protect innocent people from the monsters with motors. The same rule should apply to modern cars carrying children which can be much more lethal.

For some inexplicable reason men dominate when it comes to holiday driving, especially for distances exceeding 1000 miles without sleep. Women are relegated to the navigator role holding the map upside down or rolled up to whack heads in the back seat. All the behavioural science in the world shows just how bad an idea this is. Women can multi-task. Driving with the CD player full blast, talking into the mobile phone, checking her reflection in the courtesy mirror while simultaneously whacking blindly over her shoulder just out of reach children's brain boxes is a mere bagatelle for a woman. Prostate owners are totally different. They need to focus on one thing, a soft radio is almost acceptable but children constantly asking, 'when do we get there dad?' causes a cerebral overload and he will also start over shoulder whacking but generally with greater reach. As this all exceeds his processor's spec something has to drop out, usually the wheel turning, foot pedalling or vehicle in front avoidance stuff is the first to go.

Women should drive on holiday and men should read maps. He might be able to stretch this as far as pushing sweets into the driver's mouth while desperately looking forward through the windscreen. Unwrapping them first is an optional extra. Children,

Photo: © iStockphoto.com, Jorge Delgado

on the other hand, should be designated no useful function whatsoever. Entreaties on the autobahn such as, 'Everyone watch out for the turn-off sign for Gluckenheim' gives a margin for error only slightly better than American space probes to Mars where the manufacturer, unlike the metric scale-based NASA, worked in Imperial units. While you are working on the 'constant desperate sideways scan' scale the children are on the fixed forward gaze of 'oh God, when will all this end' units. Only five exits past the correct turn off, rapidly approaching Latvia, do you realise that the pleasant silence from behind is linked to closed eyes.

Trains

Trains are little more than a large number of Peugeot 205 cars all linked together. Instead of just your own children you are incarcerated for the duration with the genetic debris of other parents, most of whom appear to be perfectly happy with their progeny climbing into your suitcase. Any complaint over them pulling out your favourite knickers with purple hearts studded on the crotch and wearing them as balaclavas could be met with Train Rage. So you smile grimly as your own children hide in their comics muttering, 'How could mum *wear* such knickers? Worse still, how could she take them away on holiday simply to *humiliate* us all'?

Coaches

In the days of Dick Turpin it took three days to travel from London to Newcastle. On the plus side the bandits were outside of the coach. Now they seem to be driving it. Hurtling along

HELP

Italian autostrada at speeds Schumacher only dreams about you fumble in your handbag for the travel insurance documents wondering whether they will survive a head-on collision with a truck carrying twenty Fiats. More to the point, will intensive care for five exceed the hotel bill in Perugia? Modern coaches' engines are limited by governors designed to keep the vehicle speed below a set limit more often determined by optimum fuel consumption than excessive speed. Free fall down a one in four hill with the engine idling means nothing to the governor. Fortunately it reminds most children of adventure parks. 'This is *fun* mum' from your youngest, with so little life behind her.

Planes

Aeroplanes are still the safest form of transport after lifts. If this was all there was to it, fine, but simply getting into the machine is not always straightforward. Unless you are related to Bill Gates you will probably be travelling economy class. Long haul flights are just exactly what it says on the tin and like St. Peter's journey can be a religious conversion. Finally stepping out on to solid ground in Melbourne most people say, 'God that was a long haul'.

On-board entertainment includes tips on how to avoid clots in your legs from protracted immobility. Children sit next to the window. You sit at the aisle. Every hour you will exercise your calf muscles as they go to the toilet, again.

Boats

Hitler once sent a shipload of 'genetically favourable men and women' away for a cruise to bolster the 'master race'. They came

back with sea sickness rather than morning sickness and this was before they had U-boats. Cruises now tend to be for people who have absolutely no interest in producing any more members of any race, master or otherwise. Boats on the other hand are still popular with families, members of which may indeed become masters even if it is only by degree. Getting a carload of sleeping bags, sleeping children and half-sleeping parents onto a plane at Dublin Airport is never easy. By a strange twist of fate, getting exactly the same car onto a ferry at Cork harbour can be just as difficult. Roll-on roll-off ferries by definition certainly do roll. Just look at your children's green faces desperately trying to

keep breakfast one roll away from becoming flotsam and jetsam. And children really can jet some.

Bikes

Many people cycle while on holiday but some families cycle *to* their holiday. Easy to spot, the tandem has a side-car. Fathers ride at the front where mothers can check he is pedalling as hard or preferably harder than she is. Children sit grim faced while stopped at traffic lights, pretending not to notice the labrador staking its territorial claim on the side-car wheel.

Walking

Unless you live in Papua New Guinea families are unlikely to walk to their holiday. However, such is the distance between airport car park, check in and departure gates you will feel as though you have walked to Papua New Guinea before settling down in economy class. Walking in holiday cities is a different matter although it is horribly easy to get lost. If you see a family of rather short people carrying blow-pipes you missed the turning.

Trams/buses

An alternative to walking in a city is to take a tram or bus. Most now expect you to buy a ticket before boarding so carry small change at all times. The dumb foreigner routine fails to impress Milan ticket inspectors not least because the only people on the tram are dumb foreigners.

PART 7 **Accommodation**

Hotels

It's when you first see your hotel, clearly visible through the add on full building climbing frame, that you fully appreciate the adage, 'Better to travel in hope than arrive in despair'.

It is a hundred foot climbing frame with cement mixers rather than rubber impact absorbing flooring below. When you booked it from the glossy brochure it said nothing about this climbing frame or for that matter the obstacle course in what should have been the swimming pool. Choosing a hotel without seeing it is similar to a blind date in a gurning competition. Ask your friends, insist on recent photos.

For mums, hotels are a real holiday. No cooking, serving, making beds, cleaning floors or washing dishes. Everyone else complains about the lack of real gravy. Half-board gets you the gravy but no mum.

Self catering chalets

It is usually fathers who favour these little homes from home because they are cheap. Mothers can smell a stitch up from a thousand paces. Everyone will be on holiday except her because mothers cook, wash and clear up. That's why they are called mothers not fathers. As fathers are not at work they must be by definition, on holiday. Children are not at school and as they never do any housework at home, they too must also be on holiday.

Mothers, on the other hand, do not work therefore they are on holiday all the time anyway, so it is just right that they do all

Photo: © iStockphoto.com, Christopher Jones

the skivvying and waiting on for those who really are on holiday needing a well deserved break. This can lead to frayed maternal tempers. Children returning from a self catering chalet holiday are easily recognised by their bright red ears from hot saucepan lids used cymbal style in response to 'When's dinner ready mum?'

Caravans

Self catering chalets on wheels are called caravans. Everything in the previous section applies but more so. The worst thing about caravans is the fact they tend to look exactly like the kitchen back home. The reason is simple, all of the kitchen at home is now inside the caravan. Unfortunately while the kitchen is big enough to swing a cat the caravan is only just large enough to swing a small child around by the ears. Most modern caravans have their own toilets which bodes well. Beneath the toilet seat there is a large rectangular box. Imminent overflow, divorce and infanticide is indicated by a natty little red scale. With four children and two adults all consuming huge quantities of soft drinks, ice cream, beer and home made Irish stew it will dip into red within eighteen hours of arrival. Fathers empty Porta loos. That's why they are called fathers. Mothers merely use the Porta Loo because they don't want to go to the toilet block with their hair in a mess which of course it always is because mothers do all the cooking, cleaning and clearing up.

Tents

A tent is a piece of thin fabric stretched over poles. These used to be made of wood which of course swelled when wet rendering them totally impossible to dismantle.

Families can go camping. Parents of all such families are descended from Trappist monks who consider it a mortal sin to sleep on mattresses of any description. Ground is hard while people are soft. You can confirm this by jumping out of economy class while passing over your Eurocamp site at twelve thousand feet. You will probably still walk better than the poor sod waking up after a night on a deflated Lilo. Although you can hear bodily functions quite clearly through canvas the big plus tents have over caravans is, like warmth, the smell tends not to linger.

PART  **7**

Where to go with toddlers

Where in the world?

Knowing where you are going seems sensible but many children have a hazy knowledge of world geography not helped by the speed of modern transport dimming the perception of distance. Jet lag affects children just as it does adults but there is nothing to pin that strange feeling on.

So what are you looking for?

With young children it is generally best to go somewhere you already know. On the other hand families of six will wait a long time for familiar territory. Older children do take part of the brunt when it comes to dealing with the strange and unfamiliar.

- Do check the immunisations needed for entry. Go one better and seek those immunisations which will stand them in good stead in later life.
- Malaria is a very real risk. It is the single greatest cause of childhood death from infectious disease. Check if the strain in your intended holiday are resistant to the prevention on offer. Another country maybe?

- Seasons go with illness and weather. Check it out in the web search engines such as Google.
- School holidays often determine peak periods. Schools are getting increasingly twitchy about parents taking their children way from school during term time but some 'holidays' can provide more education than two weeks cramming the National Curriculum. Write or talk to the principal, there may be a way of combining your holiday with their education. Being inside an Egyptian pyramid beats the hell out of a one hour class on the Pharaohs.
- Some parts of the world are out of sync with UK and Irish school holidays. Caribbean holidays for instance are cheapest just when European destinations are at their most expensive.

Must have stuff
- Safe area, low crime rates.
- Low risk from parasitic (eg, malaria) infections.
- No spiders, snakes, insects with nasty front or back ends.
- Child-friendly people, but not too friendly.
- Acceptable medical services covered either by reciprocal agreement or basic insurance.
- Acceptable travel times.
- Beaches free from leg amputating indigenous species. *Jaws* is not recommended.
- Food that will leave neither a trail or trial.
- As good as can be hoped for from road traffic accidents.
- Parents who can cope. That's you. If you can't stand the heat don't go to the Continental kitchen.

PART

Do you have enough budgeted?

As a basic rule of thumb for budgeting a family holiday you should add up all the fares, accommodation and subsistence costs, add 20% then double it all for each child in the family. Children on holiday can seriously damage your credit rating. During the cold war the CIA offered free holidays to Soviet families in an attempt to totally bankrupt the regime. That's why it was called the Red Economy, it was always in the red.

Add up the following costs
● Flights.
● Car hire.
● Accommodation.
● Petrol/road tolls.
● Daily allowance for eating out/buying food.
● Souvenirs.
● Extra in case you need it/emergency.

Photo: © iStockphoto.com

PART  **7**

Holiday disasters

Travel companies usually give you 28 days after the end of your trip to complain, and generally the quicker you put in a travel insurance claim, the better. Holiday disasters broadly fall into three areas:

Problems with accommodation, food or flights?
Complain to your tour operator.

Lost luggage, medical bills or robbery?
Contact your travel insurer.

Unsatisfactory holiday?
Complaining about the quality of a holiday generally can be difficult, but best first approach is to the tour operator. Their complaints procedure should be set out at the back of its brochure; you should follow this and write a letter of complaint to the given address.

What to do

- State exactly what was wrong with the holiday. Don't embellish or fib.
- Be clear over what you expect the firm to do to compensate you.
- Set a deadline for reply but avoid threats.
- Keep all documents, photos, etc.
- Don't give up if your claim is initially rejected. Remain calm and polite.
- Keep copies of all correspondence and note down details of phone conversations, particularly the name of the person dealing with your complaint.

If you have reached a deadlock you can contact the travel trade association ABTA, which runs an arbitration scheme for its members, or you can take further legal action.

If your complaint is against a travel insurer, the Financial Ombudsman Service can step in once you have the firm's final response or have waited more than eight weeks for it.

Photo: © iStockphoto.com

8

PART **8**

Safety at home

PART  # Avoidable accidents

Introduction

Most car crashes happen within 100 yards of the home. With children under five, most accidents happen in the home. Like the automobile variety they occur very quickly and are more likely when adults are under stress, in a rush or when their usual routine is changed. Because you know your own home, you are in the best position to look out for possible dangers.

The kinds of accidents children have are related to their age or developmental stage so there are particular things to watch out for depending on the age of your child. Accidents range from the trivial bruise to the life-threatening burn. If a child can be distracted easily from their distress it is unlikely to be serious but never underestimate the stoicism of children, particularly when they may be feeling guilty over the accident. It can be very difficult to tell the difference between child abuse and an accident. Other children, including siblings, can be merciless and bite marks from jealous brothers or sisters are not uncommon. Don't be surprised if the doctor or nurse asks you some searching questions should you turn up at casualty. Most departments have automatic referral systems to the social services for any fracture or serious injury to children. This can be very distressing for parents and for the social workers concerned.

Under 1 year old

At this stage children are able to wriggle, grasp, suck and roll over. There are a number of possible accidents that are common in this age group.

Suffocation and choking

Young children can swallow, inhale or choke on items such as small toys, peanuts and marbles. Choose toys appropriate to the age of your child. Look for: 'contains small parts unsuitable for small children' labels. Ensure that small objects such as marbles, peanuts and small toys are kept out of reach. Encourage older children to keep their toys away from your baby. Avoid pillows and soft bedding, don't put infants to sleep unattended in an adult bed or on the sofa.

Falls

Particularly likely if you leave your child on a raised surface. Be sure, when you are changing nappies, that you avoid the child rolling off a bed or sofa. You can use a mat on the floor. This also goes for the changing rooms in supermarkets and restraints.

Burns and scalds

Possible if your child is near hot objects. Avoid hot or warm objects such as ovens, light bulbs, radiators, curling tongs, hairdryers, irons and fires. Place hot drinks out of reach. Fit short power leads on kettles and heaters. **Remember** hot water can scald up to 30 minutes after it has boiled.

Poisoning

Young children's natural instincts are to suck anything which comes into contact with their mouths. Many ordinary household substances can be poisonous, even iron tablets or salt.

All poisonous substances should be kept outside your child's reach at all times. This includes medicines such as sleeping tablets which tend to be left on the bedroom table conveniently next to the bed.

Young brothers or sisters should be supervised when around infants to stop them feeding tablets or other poisonous substances to baby just to see what happens.

1-4 years old

Once the mainframe computer kicks in with better acceleration toddlers can move very quickly, so accidents often happen in seconds. Unfortunately coordination comes later. As children get older they will explore more which means they are more likely to have knocks and bruises, not least from their adoring brothers and sisters. Keeping an eye on the wandering toddler and thinking ahead can be difficult but life-saving. Thankfully not that many kids turn up in casualty with pots stuck on their heads.

Falls

Although small children can squeeze their bodies through a gap as little as 100mm wide (smaller than the length of a teaspoon) they tend to get their heads trapped.

Check the width between railings, banisters and balconies and board them up if necessary. Fit window locks or safety catches that stop windows opening wider than 100mm.

Move furniture such as beds, sofas and chairs away from windows to prevent children climbing up and falling out.

Fit a safety gate at the bottom and top of the stairs, use a safety gate to keep small children out of the kitchen too. Make sure older children know they should keep the gate locked.

Photo: © iStockphoto.com, Brian McEntire

Burns and scalds

Any burn greater than the size of the child's hand needs the attention of a doctor. Unfortunately we do underestimate the danger from simple things like a cup of tea to a little body with such a small surface area.

Make sure that you use an appropriate fire guard for all fires. Fit a smoke alarm on each floor of your home and make sure you check that it is working properly on a weekly basis. It is a good idea to have a fire escape plan worked out and to tell your children what to do in case of a fire.

Place hot drinks out of children's reach. Fit short power leads on kettles and heaters. Use the rear hobs of the cooker, keeping pan handles turned away from the edge. Children are curious and will reach for handles of pans on the stove.

Poisoning

By the age of 18 months or earlier children can open containers and by 3 years they may also be able to open child resistant tops and child cupboard safety catches with impunity - next stop the Rubik's cube.

Keep household chemicals, medicines, alcohol and even cosmetics out of children's reach, preferably in a locked cupboard, lockable suitcase or cosmetics case.

H34147

PART **8** # Child protection

Introduction

Protecting our children from harm means more than just vaccinations. Every year one child in five has an accident at home which is serious enough to need the doctor or treatment in hospital. Most homes just aren't designed with the safety of toddlers as a first priority; the comfort and convenience of adults is the overriding factor. This can be seen when a house is up for sale. All the safety features which protect children are removed from sight just in case they should detract from the appearance of the house. Many people will take child guards away when they are expecting guests.

Designs for such things as stairs can take little regard of the probability that at some time there will be children in the house. Equally, people will accept designs for buildings to live in which ignore children because they either have none of their own or they have all grown up. Yet almost all houses will have children in them at some time; relatives, guests and visitors may all bring along their children. It is best to include the potential for such safety devices, even if they are not required immediately.

It's from the first day baby crawls (at about 9 months) up to the time a toddler learns to recognise some of the main dangers around him (at about 4 years) that your child is most at risk from an accident at home. Now that infectious diseases no longer pose such a threat (they were once the commonest cause of death for children under two years old), accidents present the greatest risk. Thankfully the loss of life and illness is not on the same scale but as most accidents are preventable, they represent a tragic game of chance for small children.

Natural curiosity, an innocent lack of fear, together with the unsteady process of learning to walk, all conspire to put toddlers at risk of injury from very ordinary, everyday things. Kettles, cups of tea, bath-water, heaters, stairs, windows, kitchen gadgets, cooking utensils, household DIY and garden chemicals, as well as the obvious hazards of medicines and drugs, all hold dangers for them.

Parents can do a great deal to reduce the risks faced by their children simply by being aware of where danger lurks. One way is to take a look round the house, room by room, to identify risks.

Many dangers can be removed at no expense. It may mean that adults have to put up with a less attractive or convenient home for a few years. But for the sake of a young child's safety and well-being surely that's a worthwhile sacrifice. Your child needs the freedom to explore your home in safety. Few would deny that bruises and sticking plaster are a natural part of growing-up, but given that most accidents in the home or garden can be prevented, serious injuries to children should be neither acceptable or probable.

Cooker guards

Some of the most horrendous injuries to children occur in the kitchen or where there is unguarded equipment. Men are already aware of the danger but as we are spending increasingly more time in the kitchen, the dangers become more immediately obvious. There is now a wide range of protective guards and equipment designed to prevent burns and scalds caused by toddlers pulling hot utensils or kitchen gadgets and their contents over them. Three-quarters of serious scalds to one to four year olds involve spillage from cups, teapots, kettles and saucepans. A minor scald to an adult from a cup of tea can be lethal to a small baby because of their small surface area of skin.

Hob and cooker guards are normally easy to fit, but fitting a hob guard to a sealed hob can be more difficult. Remember though that the guard itself, along with the sides and doors of some cookers, can get very hot. Don't get lulled into a false sense of security. After fitting a cooker or hob guard, still take care to turn pan handles away from the edge.

Electricity

Long electric flexes which overhang work tops are particularly dangerous. They can be replaced with coiled cables which will retract after stretching. When contracted they are usually about 300mm, extending to 1 metre when stretched out. Some appliances will be made safer from their use, such as: electric kettles, coffee percolators, toasters and any other small appliances, especially those where existing flex hangs over work tops to attract inquisitive fingers. However, they are not an unmixed blessing. They have the annoying and potentially dangerous habit of entangling with other flexes, particularly others of the coiled variety. It is often best not to have two coiled flexes on the same double point as there is a temptation, as happens with the telephone, not to untangle the flex until it becomes too difficult to use. Also, the very appearance of these flexes is attractive to children who are used to toys in similar designs. As an alternative, consider cordless irons and kettles. They are a good investment despite their slightly higher price.

Houses are increasingly being fitted with residual current device (RCD) circuit breakers, also known as earth leakage trips. These units will detect extremely small currents leaking to earth and break the circuit almost instantly. If a child succeeds in circumventing all your best efforts at preventing electric shock, provided there is a good earth in the house and the equipment is correctly wired, they will not be killed by the shock. Even so, there is still a contact with the electric mains even though it is only for a fraction of a second. They will receive an electric shock which could cause them to fall or drop the apparatus, thus causing injury. Preventing a shock in the first place is still the name of the game.

Safety gates and barriers

Expecting children, particularly very young children, to use their common-sense with regard to dangerous areas, is forgetting the lemming-like regard such junior members of the human race have for personal safety. Gates or barriers should be used at the threshold of any danger for an unsteady toddler or a crawling baby. They are a must to prevent a baby falling down the stairs. You may also save injuries and worry if you put them in the doorway of the kitchen, the bathroom, at the back door and the doorway to the garage or tool-shed.

Make sure that the gate or barrier you buy is approved for the use to which it will be put, but remember that no BS number will protect your child from incorrect fitting. At the top of the stairs, gates which give way when pushed are potentially more dangerous than no gate at all. Similarly, having to climb over a gate which is too difficult to open presents a danger not only to an adult but also to the child they may be carrying in their arms. Older children will usually take the easiest route and simply clamber over the gate (or swing on it). If it is right on the edge of the flight of stairs, they too can easily fall.

A gate is a permanent fixture; it needs to be screwed into the wall, banisters or door posts, which in turn need to be stout enough to take the load. But it can be opened and closed easily and quickly to allow adults and older children through. Most gates swing both ways and can be hinged either side. One model folds up concertina fashion against the wall to allow adults to get through. Avoid self-closing varieties which may well close but fail to lock. They can also close with enough force to knock a small child backwards down the stairs.

When is a gate not a gate? When it is ajar, obviously. A gate is no use at all if you forget to close it properly. Training the older children into the habit of always closing doors along with gates will help keep the younger members of the family safe.

A barrier can be moved from place to place round the home but it must be carefully tightened up every time. Nevertheless, once firmly in place, you can be sure a toddler can't get through. Both barriers and gates come in a choice of wood or metal designs. Most barriers are simple to fix. They rely on rubber buffer tension fixing, so there is no need to screw anything into the walls or posts at each end. You may find barriers with only one buffer (rather than two) at each end more convenient.

Guards for heaters and fires

Children, like all animals, are fascinated by fire. For the stone-age father, it must have been a constant worry that Ug junior was about to fall into the flames. Sadly, injuries from fires still account for a very large proportion of childhood hospital visits. Strong, well-attached guards should be used anywhere there is a gas or electric heater, an open fire, wood or oil burning stove. Avoid the flimsy free-standing guards which are designed for appearance rather than their ability to protect. Look for a big all-round guard to protect toddlers both from the fire itself and from the hot casing or surround. Do not rely on the metal bars attached to the heater to protect your toddler; they can get very hot.

Open fires need the extra protection of a spark guard inside the main fire guard, but beware, spark guards themselves can get very hot. Bathing your baby in front of the fire is very pleasant but this too requires the use of a spark guard and a reasonable distance between the bath and the fire.

Portable heaters are particularly dangerous, so make sure they are well inside a guard which is fixed to the wall. For mobile gas cylinder heaters, use one of the guards designed specifically for them. Ideally, no part of the guard should be closer than 200mm from the heat source. Too close and the guard itself could get dangerously hot.

Window locks

Many landings in older houses have windows at floor or near floor level. It makes sense to protect these windows from children while at the same time allowing their use for ventilation and as fire escapes. Locks are better, therefore, than vertical bars because so long as you keep the key handy, the window can still provide an escape route if there's a fire.

If you don't like the idea of no fresh air in the room, consider those locks which can also set the window in a slightly open position. (The maximum safe opening for children is about 100mm) Even windows apparently out of reach can be a danger to children if there is furniture under windows for children to climb on to.

Having fire-practice drills can be great fun for the children. It establishes a pattern for them should there be a fire. It also helps identify those windows which will not open any more, usually after the last round of house painting.

Safety glass and film

Building regulations now dictate that all new houses, or glass replacement where children can reach, must be of a minimum thickness to prevent children from falling through the glass. It is difficult to overemphasise just how serious injury to children can be from such an accident. Unfortunately, even the thicker glass is not unbreakable and the glass will leave pointed fragments within the frame. Safety glass is not only stronger than ordinary glass, but when it does break up it is much less likely to cause serious injury. Choose between laminated glass and toughened (tempered) safety glass.

Laminated glass is made from two sheets of ordinary glass with a sheet of plastic sandwiched and bonded between them. When it is damaged it stays in one piece, the glass being held together by the plastic inside. It can be cut and trimmed to size but not as easily as ordinary glass.

Safety film is a clear plastic film which is spread on to one surface of the existing glass in your home. It holds the glass together if it gets broken. Safety film is difficult to remove once properly in place. Safety film is cheaper than safety glass, but is less effective, particularly if incorrectly fitted. Both methods of protection are also useful as burglar deterrents but have the serious disadvantage of making escape from fire difficult if the window needs to be broken.

Medicines and dangerous chemicals

Every year a considerable number of children will eat, drink or pour medicine and chemicals over themselves. Children are naturally curious. It's a healthy instinct but unless you take precautions to keep dangerous things beyond their reach, there could be distinctly unhealthy results. Poisoning is one of the most common accidents amongst children between one and four years old.

The treatment necessary to save poison victims can be very frightening for toddlers. Washing out the stomach by passing a tube down their throat is standard for the non-toxic chemicals. Similarly, an emetic (a substance which makes them vomit) is often employed while they are fully conscious. For most forms of poisoning, blood samples will need to be taken. So it make sense to keep all drugs, pills and medicines, as well as household and garden chemicals, in child-resistant containers or firmly behind closed cupboard doors which children cannot open. Child resistant catches are cheap and easy to fit. It may be safer to keep garden and DIY chemicals under lock and key in the garden shed or garage.

Because medicines and drugs hold particular dangers for toddlers (pills look like sweets, medicines look like juice) you may want to keep all medicines, etc, in a lockable cabinet as a first priority.

One of the commonest causes of poisoning involves keeping dangerous chemicals such as weed-killers in lemonade bottles. You should never transfer chemicals from the bottles or packets they are sold in.

House fires

About 80 children die in house fires every year. This is the commonest cause of accidental death in the home for children.

H34148

Your local fire station will help you with advice on fire prevention and planning fire escape. Your first priority if a fire occurs is to get everyone out as quickly as possible and not to try to put the fire out yourself. Once out of the house children should be kept somewhere safe and no attempt made to return inside the house. Many families have lost their father for the sake of a favourite toy or TV set.

A well-placed smoke detector alarm on every floor will wake you in the event of a fire. It will only do this, however, if it has power to work it. You should pick one day per week to check the batteries, turning it into a game for the children helps spread the load. Better still, install units which permanently charge from the mains. Even so, they will still need to be checked on a regular basis.

Sitting and playing

It seems incredible that many accidents and injury to chidlren occur during 'play-time'. It is often not the type of play which is the danger but rather the lack of supervision or the equipment being used in an inappropriate manner. Some play equipment has been found to be dangerous and is no longer recommended. This is particularly true of the baby walker – many of these items can, however, still be bought, particularly second-hand, and may even carry a BS number.

PART 9 Childhood ailments

PART  # General

Introduction

Most accidental injuries are minor and can be treated using simple first aid measures, but in the unlikely event of a serious accident or sudden illness, knowledge of first aid techniques could help you to save your child's life. You should get professional training rather than waiting for it to happen first.

By following the basic guidelines provided here you will be able to deal with most day-to-day accidents and injuries. Information on dealing with emergencies is also provided.

To get more detailed information, and training in emergency first aid, contact the British Red Cross or St John Ambulance (see *Contacts* on page 183).

The key things to remember in any emergency situation are:
- Remain calm and confident.
- Do all you can to help but don't put yourself in danger.
- Do not give the injured person anything to eat or drink.

Emergencies

Seek **URGENT** medical attention for:
- Head injury with bleeding from eyes, ears or nose, drowsiness or vomiting.
- Loss of consciousness.
- Broken bone or dislocation.
- Severe chest pain or breathlessness.
- Sudden severe abdominal pain that won't go away.
- Unresolved choking and difficulty breathing.
- Severe bleeding.

Getting help

Sometimes, the quickest way of getting medical help is to take the child directly to the accident department of your local hospital. But call an ambulance and do not move the child if:
- You think they have a back or neck injury, or any other injury that could be made worse by movement.
- The child is unconscious or has stopped breathing, and needs your constant attention.

PART 9 How to deal with an emergency

The recovery position

This is a safe position for an unconscious casualty, which allows easy breathing and prevents choking if they vomit.

After checking they are breathing normally, turn them on their side. Ensure that the airway is clear, with the jaw pulled forward and their head tipped slightly back.

Mouth-to-mouth resuscitation (kiss of life)

Note: *There is a risk of damaging an infant's lungs by blowing into the mouth. Better to let your chest fall naturally without forcing the breath out.*

Check first for anything obstructing the airway inside the mouth.

- Place the child on a firm surface. Tilt back the head and lift the chin to open the air passages.
- Check for 10 seconds to see if they are breathing. If they are, place them in the recovery position described above.
- Cover the mouth and nose with your mouth (or just the nose if you cannot make a good seal) and give a gentle breath. Their chest should rise.
- Allow their chest to fall and give five more breaths (at about 20 per minute).
- Check whether they are breathing on their own. If not, continue.

Cardio-pulmonary resuscitation (CPR)

If there is still no breathing, start CPR.

- Place the child in the same position as for mouth-to-mouth resuscitation.
- Imagine a line between the child's nipples. Place one hand just below the mid-point of this line.
- Press at the rate of 100 per minute (in time with 'Nelly the Elephant'), moving the chest down no more than 30mm with each press.
- Give 30 compressions to 2 mouth-to-mouth breaths.

While you are doing this, someone else should be telephoning 999/112 for an ambulance. Keep other important numbers readily available.

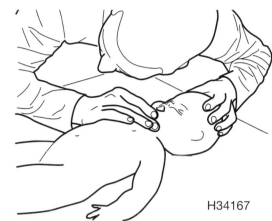

Tilt back the head and lift the chin to open the air passages

H34167

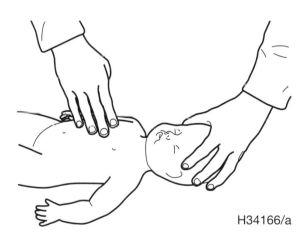

CPR point

H34166/a

PART 9 Is your toddler really ill?

Parents are usually good at noticing when something is wrong with their toddler, but it is common not to be sure whether there is something really wrong.

Look out for these important signs and call your doctor or NHS Direct (0845 46 47).

Something wrong with the toddlery's response to you such as:

- When awake, your child may seem unusually drowsy or not interested in looking at you.
- Not interested in feeding.
- When cuddled, your toddler feels floppy or limp.
- Crying seems different (perhaps moaning, whimpering or shrill), and soothing doesn't help.

Other signs of illness

If you are already worried and then notice other problems too (like those in the list below), call your doctor or NHS Direct (0845 46 47) for advice.

- Is your toddler very pale?
- Is your toddler irritable and does not like being touched?
- Is there a new rash starting to appear?
- Is there bruised or discoloured look to the skin?
- Is there a fever?
- Is there difficulty with breathing or is breathing much faster than usual?
- Is your toddler being sick (vomiting)?

A fever can be a sign that something is wrong. Anything over 38°C (100°F) is cause for concern

Photo: © iStockphoto.com, Monika Adamczyk

PART 9 Taking a young child to hospital

If you and your child need to go to hospital:

- Reassure your child and explain that you're going together to see the doctor at the hospital to make things better.
- Take a favourite toy with you.
- Dress your child in a coat or a dressing gown over their nightclothes, or dress your child fully (it doesn't matter which, do what seems most sensible).
- Arrange care for other children or, if this is not possible, take them as well (it is not wise to leave a child at home without an adult there to look after them).

Photo: © iStockphoto.com, Trista Weibell

PART  **Antibiotics**

Introduction

In the vast majority of cases, children will get better without antibiotics, so it makes sense for your doctor not to prescribe them. Their body's defence system can often protect against infection without the need for antibiotics which are being prescribed far too much.

Don't always expect to be given a prescription as doctors need to prescribe antibiotics with care, not least because inappropriate use of antibiotics can be dangerous for individual patients and for the whole population. Overuse of antibiotics can also cause resistance and result in them not working in the future. This is a very worrying trend, especially for patients with serious life-threatening infections.

Antibiotic facts

- Antibiotics have no effect on viral infections (eg colds, flu and most sore throats). Viral infections are much more common than bacterial infections.
- Inappropriate use of antibiotics can encourage the development of resistant bacteria. This could mean that the antibiotic may not work when your child really needs it.
- Some antibiotics have harmful side-effects such as diarrhoea and allergic reactions.
- Antibiotics do not just attack the infection they are prescribed for, they can also kill useful bacteria which protect against other infections such as thrush.

There are effective alternative remedies for managing the symptoms of many infections.

If your child is prescribed antibiotics, ensure that they are given the medication according to instructions.

Although they may begin to feel better, they must take the full course of antibiotics to prevent their illness coming back.

Not taking the full course of antibiotics may lead to future antibiotic resistance.

If there is an infection such as a cold, flu or sore throat:

- Give paracetamol or paediatric ibuprofen according to the instructions to help reduce fever and relieve aches and pains.
- Give plenty of water to avoid dehydration.
- Ask your pharmacist (chemist) for advice. Many infections can be managed effectively with over-the-counter medications. The pharmacist will refer you to your doctor or practice nurse if they think it is necessary.

When to contact your GP

Call your GP's surgery for advice if, after taking over-the-counter medications as directed, your child is experiencing any of the following:

- Symptoms which are severe or unusually prolonged.
- Shortness of breath.
- Coughing up of blood or large amounts of yellow or green phlegm.

Harmful side-effects

Potential side-effects are another reason why doctors are cautious about prescribing antibiotics. Some antibiotic treatment can cause side-effects such as stomach upset and thrush. More serious side-effects which can be life-threatening can also happen.

Digestion problems

Gastroenteritis

Gastroenteritis simply means an inflammation of the stomach and the intestine which may cause vomiting and diarrhoea. Fortunately these attacks do tend to clear up on their own, but if the diarrhoea and vomiting are severe, dehydration can occur which can be serious, particularly in a toddler.

Symptoms

Obviously a young child cannot tell you about the pain that gastroenteritis can cause although they will tend to cry persistently. There is often a high temperature along with diarrhoea and vomiting, which can lead to serious dehydration if prolonged. If the toddler still has open gaps in the skull bones (the soft areas of the scalp – fontanelles) these may be sunken when felt with your finger tip. In the older baby or child you may notice dark concentrated urine, a furred tongue and general malaise.

Causes

Viruses such as rotaviruses, commonly found in infected shellfish, are a common cause in the older child. Bacteria and other organisms can also cause gastroenteritis. These can be picked up from contaminated food or water and may reflect poor hygiene during food preparation. Not all cases of diarrhoea when away on holiday to another country are actually 'gastroenteritis'. The organisms which normally live in our bowels and do no harm are often replaced by the 'local' variety and diarrhoea can occur during this phase.

Failing to sterilise a baby's bottle correctly or making up the feed without taking care over hygiene can cause gastroenteritis. Contrary to popular myth, microwave ovens are not a good way of sterilising bottles unless used with a steriliser specifically designed for this method.

Diagnosis

Generally this is fairly obvious and is based on the symptoms, but any sign of dehydration in children must be acted on quickly (see *Fever* on page 177, *Diarrhoea* on page 145 and *Vomiting* on page 147).

Treatment and prevention

The name of the game is to replace lost fluids so diluting feeds, allowing more and longer feeds or giving rehydration mixtures as advised by your doctor helps replace lost fluid in young children and babies. If they are unable to take fluids for any reason such as repeated vomiting you should call your doctor. Do not give fizzy drinks, even after allowing them to go flat, as the sugar content can actually make the symptoms worse.

Anti-diarrhoeal medicine should not be given to young children. Some may be dangerous. Antibiotics are of no value in most cases of gastroenteritis, particularly those caused by viruses, and indeed can even make things worse.

Worms

Unfortunately common, particularly in young children, worms are not a sign of poor hygiene or bad living. Threadworms are the most common type of worm and cause itchy bottoms but are actually harmless. Roundworms are larger but less common. Tapeworms are much less common but can still be found in some parts of the UK.

Symptoms

Threadworms or roundworms can be seen in the baby's or child's motions as tiny white/brown worms in the stool. Night-time is the worst for itchiness as the female lays its eggs at the anus at this time causing the child to scratch, pick up the eggs, and pass them on or re-infect themselves.

Causes

Worms spread very quickly once within a family and can remain in families for considerable periods of time without anybody realising it. They usually infect children from contact with another child, who then passes it on to the other members of the family. Treating the whole family makes good sense therefore.

Prevention

- Wash your children's hands after using the potty or toilet as well as your own.
- Wash their and your hands before eating.
- Wash their and your hands after handling animals.

Treatment and self care

Use inverted adhesive tape (as you would for removing fluff from a jacket) to pick up worms or eggs from around the child's back passage. Bring it with you to your doctor who will prescribe medicine which works very effectively.

Abdominal pain

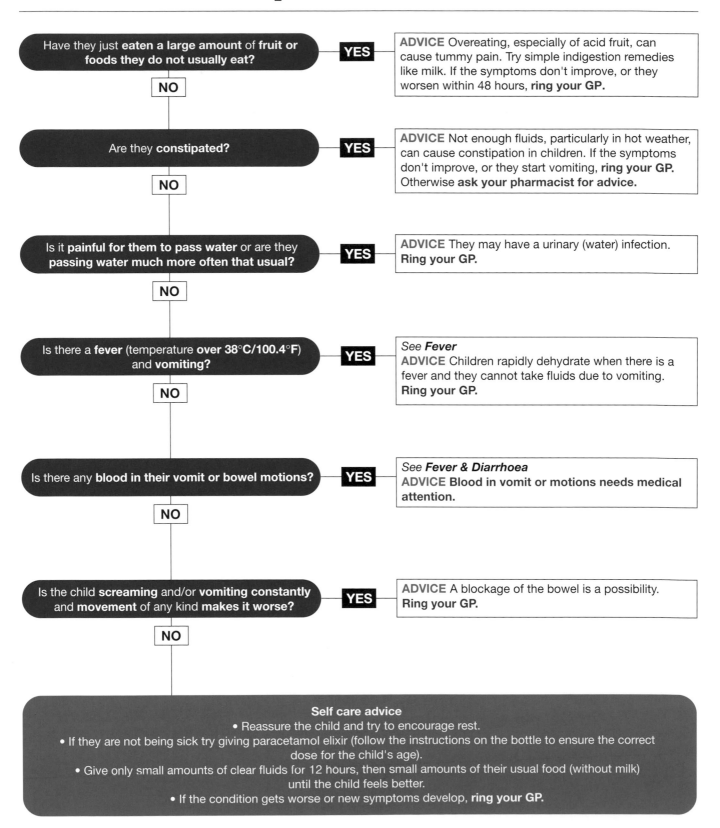

Have they just **eaten a large amount** of **fruit or foods they do not usually eat?**

YES → **ADVICE** Overeating, especially of acid fruit, can cause tummy pain. Try simple indigestion remedies like milk. If the symptoms don't improve, or they worsen within 48 hours, **ring your GP.**

NO ↓

Are they **constipated?**

YES → **ADVICE** Not enough fluids, particularly in hot weather, can cause constipation in children. If the symptoms don't improve, or they start vomiting, **ring your GP.** Otherwise **ask your pharmacist for advice.**

NO ↓

Is it **painful for them to pass water** or are they **passing water much more often that usual?**

YES → **ADVICE** They may have a urinary (water) infection. **Ring your GP.**

NO ↓

Is there a **fever** (temperature **over 38°C/100.4°F**) and **vomiting?**

YES → *See **Fever*** **ADVICE** Children rapidly dehydrate when there is a fever and they cannot take fluids due to vomiting. **Ring your GP.**

NO ↓

Is there any **blood in their vomit or bowel motions?**

YES → *See **Fever & Diarrhoea*** **ADVICE** Blood in vomit or motions needs medical attention.

NO ↓

Is the child **screaming** and/or **vomiting constantly** and **movement** of any kind **makes it worse?**

YES → **ADVICE** A blockage of the bowel is a possibility. **Ring your GP.**

NO ↓

Self care advice
- Reassure the child and try to encourage rest.
- If they are not being sick try giving paracetamol elixir (follow the instructions on the bottle to ensure the correct dose for the child's age).
- Give only small amounts of clear fluids for 12 hours, then small amounts of their usual food (without milk) until the child feels better.
- If the condition gets worse or new symptoms develop, **ring your GP.**

Diarrhoea

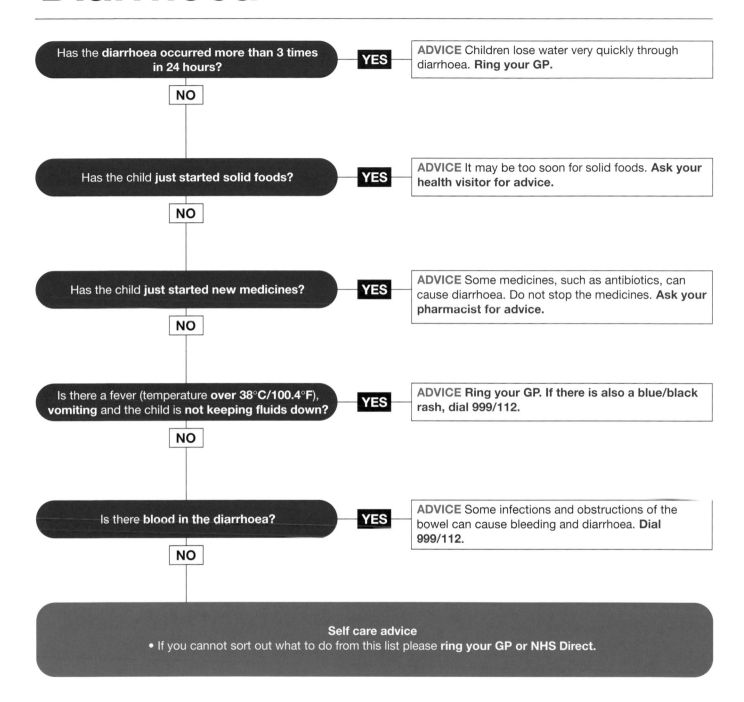

Has the diarrhoea occurred more than 3 times in 24 hours?

YES → **ADVICE** Children lose water very quickly through diarrhoea. **Ring your GP.**

NO

Has the child just started solid foods?

YES → **ADVICE** It may be too soon for solid foods. **Ask your health visitor for advice.**

NO

Has the child just started new medicines?

YES → **ADVICE** Some medicines, such as antibiotics, can cause diarrhoea. Do not stop the medicines. **Ask your pharmacist for advice.**

NO

Is there a fever (temperature over 38°C/100.4°F), vomiting and the child is not keeping fluids down?

YES → **ADVICE Ring your GP. If there is also a blue/black rash, dial 999/112.**

NO

Is there blood in the diarrhoea?

YES → **ADVICE** Some infections and obstructions of the bowel can cause bleeding and diarrhoea. **Dial 999/112.**

NO

Self care advice
• If you cannot sort out what to do from this list please **ring your GP or NHS Direct.**

Poisoning

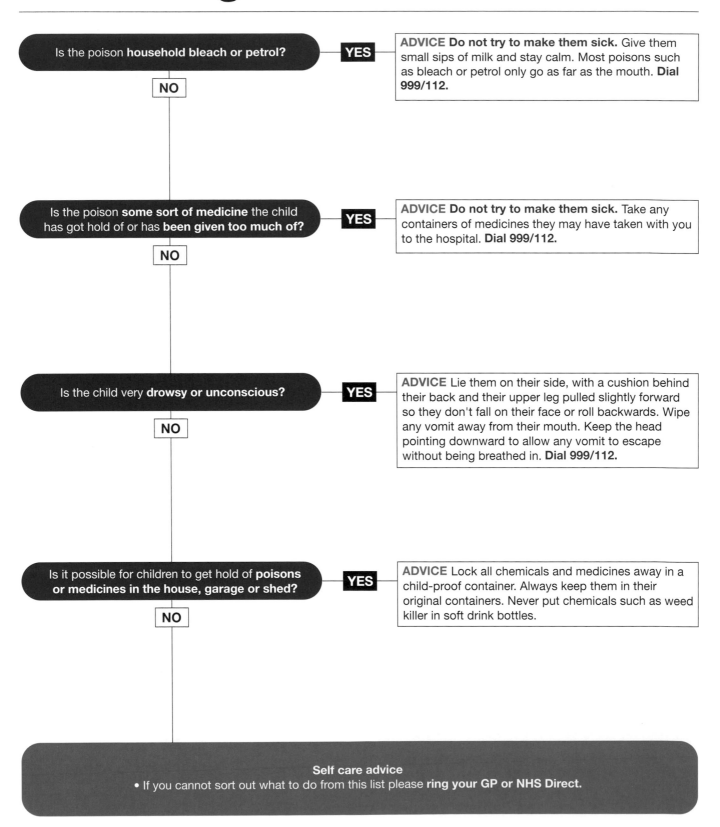

Is the poison **household bleach or petrol?**

YES → **ADVICE Do not try to make them sick.** Give them small sips of milk and stay calm. Most poisons such as bleach or petrol only go as far as the mouth. **Dial 999/112.**

NO ↓

Is the poison **some sort of medicine** the child has got hold of or has **been given too much of?**

YES → **ADVICE Do not try to make them sick.** Take any containers of medicines they may have taken with you to the hospital. **Dial 999/112.**

NO ↓

Is the child very **drowsy or unconscious?**

YES → **ADVICE** Lie them on their side, with a cushion behind their back and their upper leg pulled slightly forward so they don't fall on their face or roll backwards. Wipe any vomit away from their mouth. Keep the head pointing downward to allow any vomit to escape without being breathed in. **Dial 999/112.**

NO ↓

Is it possible for children to get hold of **poisons or medicines in the house, garage or shed?**

YES → **ADVICE** Lock all chemicals and medicines away in a child-proof container. Always keep them in their original containers. Never put chemicals such as weed killer in soft drink bottles.

NO ↓

Self care advice
• If you cannot sort out what to do from this list please **ring your GP or NHS Direct.**

Vomiting

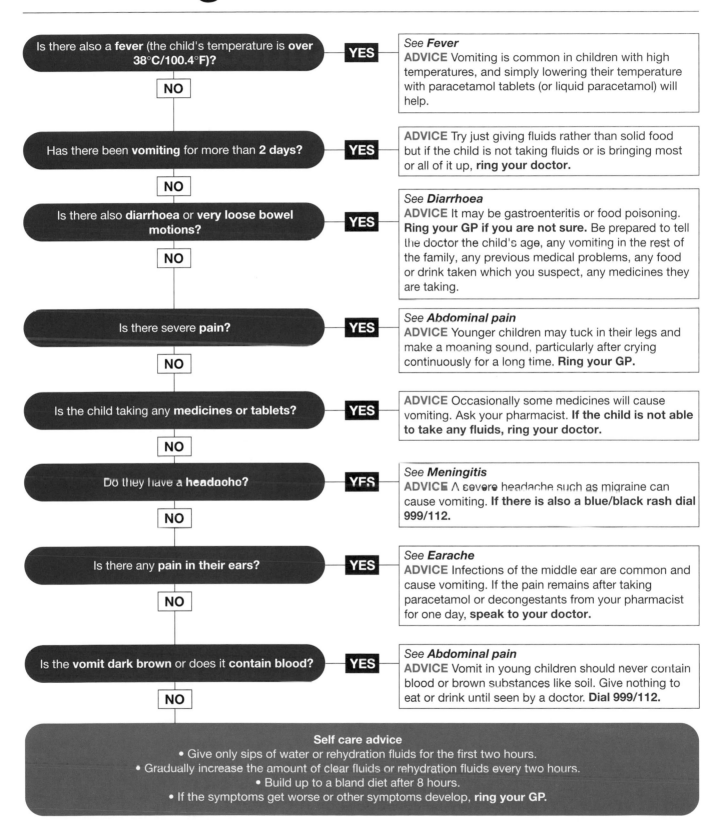

Is there also a **fever** (the child's temperature is **over 38°C/100.4°F)?** — **YES**

See *Fever*
ADVICE Vomiting is common in children with high temperatures, and simply lowering their temperature with paracetamol tablets (or liquid paracetamol) will help.

NO

Has there been **vomiting** for more than **2 days?** — **YES**

ADVICE Try just giving fluids rather than solid food but if the child is not taking fluids or is bringing most or all of it up, **ring your doctor.**

NO

Is there also **diarrhoea** or **very loose bowel motions?** — **YES**

See *Diarrhoea*
ADVICE It may be gastroenteritis or food poisoning. **Ring your GP if you are not sure.** Be prepared to tell the doctor the child's age, any vomiting in the rest of the family, any previous medical problems, any food or drink taken which you suspect, any medicines they are taking.

NO

Is there severe **pain?** — **YES**

See *Abdominal pain*
ADVICE Younger children may tuck in their legs and make a moaning sound, particularly after crying continuously for a long time. **Ring your GP.**

NO

Is the child taking any **medicines or tablets?** — **YES**

ADVICE Occasionally some medicines will cause vomiting. Ask your pharmacist. **If the child is not able to take any fluids, ring your doctor.**

NO

Do they have a **headache?** — **YES**

See *Meningitis*
ADVICE A severe headache such as migraine can cause vomiting. **If there is also a blue/black rash dial 999/112.**

NO

Is there any **pain in their ears?** — **YES**

See *Earache*
ADVICE Infections of the middle ear are common and cause vomiting. If the pain remains after taking paracetamol or decongestants from your pharmacist for one day, **speak to your doctor.**

NO

Is the **vomit dark brown** or does it **contain blood?** — **YES**

See *Abdominal pain*
ADVICE Vomit in young children should never contain blood or brown substances like soil. Give nothing to eat or drink until seen by a doctor. **Dial 999/112.**

NO

Self care advice
- Give only sips of water or rehydration fluids for the first two hours.
- Gradually increase the amount of clear fluids or rehydration fluids every two hours.
- Build up to a bland diet after 8 hours.
- If the symptoms get worse or other symptoms develop, **ring your GP.**

PART 9 Breathing problems

Asthma

For reasons we are not sure of, asthma is on the increase. Part of the problem may be pollution in our environment, particularly exhaust fumes. Thankfully deaths from asthma attacks are declining, but with around 2000 deaths each year, many in children, it should be taken very seriously. It can appear at any stage in life but is more common in children. Modern treatments will prevent or stop the vast majority of asthma attacks and it is rare in very young children. Most asthma sufferers simply have mild symptoms and may never suffer a serious attack.

Symptoms

The first sign of an attack can be as simple as a repeated cough, which can rapidly develop into a frightening breathlessness and tightness in the chest. This is usually painless, but after an attack there may be muscle strain which can ache. In the early stages a wheeze can be heard as the child breaths out. If they are suffering from a very serious attack there may be little or no wheeze or even the sound of breathing. They tend to sit up straight with their head slightly back with pursed lips. With severe attacks their lips may turn blue and they will be unable to speak. This is an emergency and you must dial 999/112.

Causes

Some forms of asthma are triggered (although not caused) by things like pollen, hay or house dust. Other forms seem to just happen with no apparent reason, although stress or a recent chest infection can act as triggers. Children who have hay fever or other allergies in the family are most likely to develop asthma.

Prevention

There is as yet no way of preventing the condition, but you can reduce the number and severity of attacks, particularly for a child with the allergic type of asthma. Keep a record of when and where they were with each attack. You may find it ties in with the presence of a particular pet, the pollen count on that day or even what they had to eat. Some of these things cannot be changed, but simple things like covering mattresses with a plastic cover to prevent dust mites, or keeping certain flowers out of the house, may make a difference. House dust mite faeces (droppings) are a powerful trigger for some asthma sufferers. Many vacuum cleaners can now be fitted with special filters which prevent these being blown into the air.

Complications

Badly-controlled asthma can be dangerous, especially if the early warning signs are ignored.

Treatment and self care

Nebulisers are sometimes supplied by the GP practice on a loan basis or from support groups. They can be useful for very young children who find hand-held inhalers difficult to use and can stop asthma attacks very rapidly. A device known as a spacer may also be used. In an emergency away from such machines, cut the large round end off a plastic lemonade bottle and fire the inhaler into the open end while the child breathes through the narrow screw-top hole.

Staying calm is vital when dealing with a child suffering an asthma attack. Remember the following points:
- Find their inhaler and help them use it.
- Dial 999/112 if it is a serious attack.
- Reassure them.
- Give them nothing to drink.
- Allow them to sit in any position they find most comfortable.
- Do not force them to lie down.
- If there is a nebuliser or spacer available, use it sooner rather than later.

Photo: © iStockphoto.com, Chris Rogers

Bronchiolitis

This condition of the lungs is very common and can lead to many hospital admissions. It is more common during the winter months and in boys. It mainly affects children up to two years old, with most cases happening at around six months old.

Cause

A virus called Respiratory Syncytial Virus (RSV) is often to blame (there is RSV positive and RSV negative bronchiolitis). It makes the small airways or bronchioles in the lungs narrow and fill with mucus, making breathing difficult. Although it usually lasts around seven days, it can also leave a lingering cough for weeks afterwards.

Signs and symptoms

An irritating cough is common but wheezing is usually the first sign. This obviously makes feeding more difficult for the baby. A fever is also often present. It is generally self-limiting and will clear up on its own, but you should ring your doctor if there is any sudden difficulty in breathing following a cough or cold, such as rapid breathing or wheezing, especially if there is also excessive drowsiness.

Treatment and self care

Admission to hospital is needed only in the most severe cases where the baby's breathing is badly affected and may require oxygen therapy and fluids.

Mild cases can be treated at home:

- Raise the head of the cot to make breathing easier at night.
- Hang damp towels on the radiator to raise the humidity in the nursery (but take care not to cause a fire hazard – check the radiator first. You may not be able to put anything on top of it). Alternatively, use a room humidifier, making sure it is out of the baby's reach.
- Make sure the baby is taking plenty of fluids.
- Nose drops can actually make things worse if you use them too often for too long. Take your doctor's advice on their use.

Choking

Choking happens surprisingly often. Immediate action is vital, so it is important to know the correct steps to follow:

- Check inside the mouth, and remove any obstruction.
- If you can't see or feel any obstruction, bend them over your hand or lap and give them 5 taps (not hard slaps) between their shoulder blades.
- If there is no response, turn them over and using two fingers only press firmly in their breast bone five times.
- If the blockage is not completely cleared, or the child continues to have trouble breathing, start again while someone seeks urgent medical attention.

Croup

Children between the ages of three months and six years are most likely to suffer from this condition which produces a seal-like barking cough which sounds terrible but is actually rarely serious. The symptoms usually lasts from three to seven days. As bad luck would have it, the cough is invariably worse during the night.

Causes
Thick mucus at the back of throat follows the initial viral infection.

Prevention
There is no known prevention for croup.

Self care
Croup can be treated by steam inhalation and does not need antibiotics. Stay calm. Getting upset will only make matters worse. If you have a bathroom, fill the bath with hot water so it steams. Alternatively run the shower on full heat with the shower door open. Otherwise choose a room which is safe to run a kettle to produce lots of steam. Simply sit with your child, allowing them to breath the warm steam in the room but not directly from the bath, shower or kettle.

Note
Inhaling a peanut or other small piece of food will produce the same kind of shortness of breath. If your child coughs and has a problem with their breathing while eating, take them to your hospital's Accident & Emergency department.

A serious but now very rare condition called epiglottitis (inflammation of the flap that closes the airway during swallowing) can be confused with croup. Fortunately the symptoms are not the same. Children with epiglottitis tend to drool while tilting their heads forward. They may have a fever and protrude their jaw as they try to breathe. Epiglottitis is caused by the same bacteria which causes one type of meningitis and has become less common since the introduction of the Hib vaccination, clearly showing the value of immunisations.

Croup can be treated by steam inhalation

H34154

Breathing difficulties

Are the **lips tinged blue** or your child **cannot speak?** — **YES** → ADVICE **Dial 999/112.**

NO

Is the child **wheezing?** — **YES** → ADVICE **Dial 999/112.**

NO

Did the difficulty follow some **food** like bread or peanuts **going 'down the wrong way'?** — **YES** → ADVICE **Dial 999/112.**

NO

Did the breathing difficulty start after **taking medicine** or **being bitten** or **stung by an insect?** — **YES** → ADVICE **Dial 999/112.**

NO

Is there also a fever, is your child flushed, feels hot and is sweaty (your child's temperature **over 38°C/100.4°F)?** — **YES** → See *Fever*
ADVICE **Call NHS Direct or your doctor.**

NO

Self care advice
- Breathing difficulties in children should not be ignored.
- If your child has asthma, make sure they take their inhalers (bronchodilators) as prescribed and **call NHS Direct** who will help to determine the urgency of your child's condition.
- If the condition gets worse or new symptoms develop, **call NHS Direct.**
- If you are still worried **call NHS Direct.**

Coughing

Is the cough **worse at night when people light up cigarettes?**	**YES**	**ADVICE** assive smoking affects children even if they are not in the same room as you, especially if they already have some other condition like a cold or asthma. **Either smoke outside or give it up.**
NO		
Does the child have **asthma?**	**YES**	*See Asthma* **ADVICE** oughing is common in asthma. **If there are any breathing difficulties, the child cannot speak, the lips are blue or they are not responding to the inhaler, dial 999/112.**
NO		
Is there also **a runny nose, sore throat, fever** (temperature **over 38°C/100.4°F**) and **general aches and pains** or **sneezing?**	**YES**	**ADVICE** It is probably a cold or flu. *See Colds and flu* **Ask your pharmacist for advice.**
NO		
Does the child **vomit after a bout of coughing** with **a whooping noise** and has **not been immunised against whooping cough?**	**YES**	**ADVICE** It is could be whooping cough (pertussis). Give paracetamol, and ice lollies; put a bowl of water in the room to humidify the air. Antibiotics or other medicines have little effect. **Ring your GP.**
NO		
Did the coughing follow **a fit of coughing after food** such as a peanut or bread **'going down the wrong way'?**	**YES**	**ADVICE** An obstruction of the airways will cause this kind of coughing. *See Breathing difficulties*. **If there is also a shortness of breath dial 999/112.**
NO		
Is there any **blood in their phlegm?**	**YES**	**ADVICE** Repeated coughing can commonly cause small blood vessels to burst but **check with your doctor.**
NO		
Is there also **difficulty in breathing or are the lips blue?**	**YES**	**ADVICE** or whatever reason (see *Breathing difficulties*), the child is not getting enough air, **dial 999/112.**
NO		

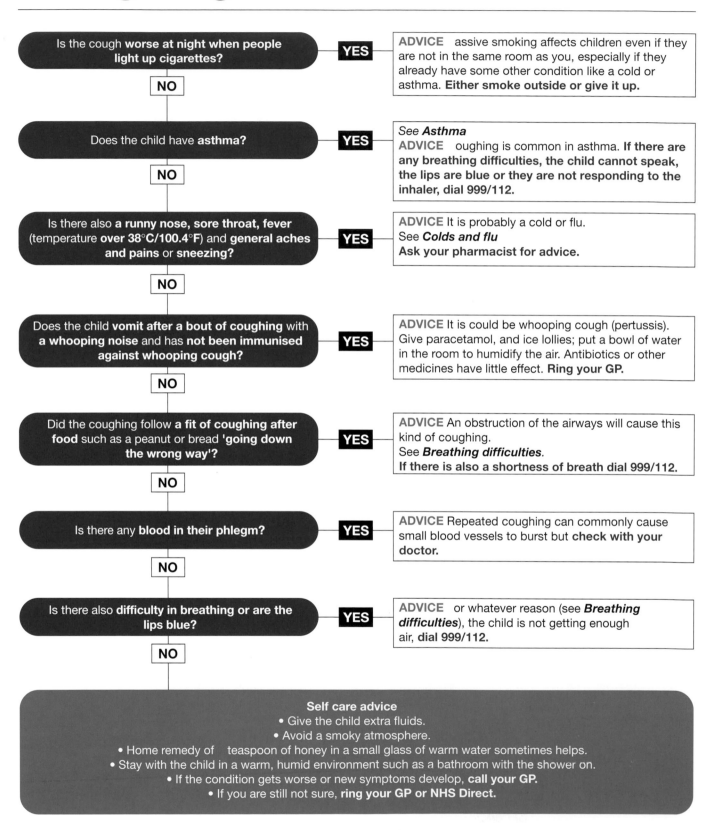

Self care advice
- Give the child extra fluids.
- Avoid a smoky atmosphere.
- Home remedy of teaspoon of honey in a small glass of warm water sometimes helps.
- Stay with the child in a warm, humid environment such as a bathroom with the shower on.
- If the condition gets worse or new symptoms develop, **call your GP.**
- If you are still not sure, **ring your GP or NHS Direct.**

PART 9 Skin problems

Bites and stings

Insects

Insect bites and stings can be painful but they are not usually serious, even in children. Most can be treated with simple, common-sense remedies without needing the attention of your doctor.

Causes

Midges, horse flies, bees, wasps, centipedes, ants, etc. The list is long, but thankfully there are no killers within the UK.

Symptoms

At first you may mistake the marks for something more serious. Looking very closely you may be able to see the small hole of the bite. The 'spot' is invariably itchy and may swell, particularly if it came from a horse fly (clegg).

Prevention

Insect repellents work. Use a mosquito net around the bed when in infested areas, particularly for children.

Treatment and self care

Although itchy and sometimes painful, insect bites and stings are rarely dangerous and need only some antihistamine or local anaesthetic cream from your pharmacist.

Initially, apply a cold compress to insect bites and stings. Remove bee stings with tweezers by gripping the base of the sting nearest to the skin to avoid squeezing the poison sac which may still contain some venom. Remove ticks by covering them with a smear of petroleum jelly, which blocks their breathing holes, and causes them to drop off. Simply pulling at the tick or trying to burn it off can leave the head in the skin, leading to infection.

Seek medical attention if:
● There is a known allergy to bites and stings.
● The sting or tick cannot be removed.
● There is infection around the site.
● There is a fever or shortness of breath.

Complications

Some children are strongly allergic to bites and stings and can be very ill. If there is any shortage of breath, dial 999/112. Bites can become infected by scratching.

Animals

Animal bites need urgent medical attention, as they may become infected if not treated. Small animal bites should be thoroughly cleaned with soap and water and covered with a sterile dressing. For serious bites, apply direct pressure with a clean cloth to control the bleeding and seek assistance.

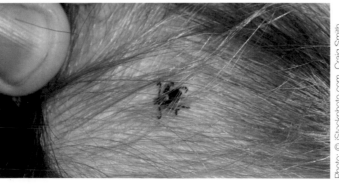

Photo: © iStockphoto.com, Craig Smith

Eczema

This skin condition can vary from being merely a nuisance to posing serious risks to the baby or child. It is more common in children and is basically an inflammation of the skin producing dry flaky patches, usually on the inside of joints such as the elbow. It is normally a mild condition.

Symptoms

There are various types of eczema but in the baby the inherited form (atopic eczema) is the most common. Children with eczema tend also to suffer from allergies such as hay fever in later life. Seborrhoeic dermatitis is the name for eczema that affects the scalp, otherwise known as cradle cap, and this is not an indication of any future problems with allergies (see *Cradle cap* on page 158).

Causes

Unfortunately the cause is unknown, but it does tend to run in families.

Treatment

Keeping the skin moist with emollient ointments is important, and your doctor or pharmacist will advise you. Steroid creams can have a dramatic effect on the severe forms of eczema, not least in preventing scarring. Unfortunately they can make the skin more prone to infection and may cause thinning of the skin with constant use. Prolonged use with absorption of the steroid can also cause metabolic problems later in life. Only use them under your doctor's direction.

Photo: © iStockphoto.com, Steve Wilson

Lice

Wherever there is hair there can be lice and they have no respect for age when it comes to taking up squatters' rights. They are small, six-legged wingless insects, pin-head size when they hatch, less than match-head size when fully grown and grey/brown in colour. Nits are egg sacs, often empty, which hatch between 7 and 10 days after laying. Nits may still be found even after all the lice have been cleared. This doesn't necessarily mean there are live lice in the hair.

Photo: © iStockphoto.com

Symptoms
Lice are embarrassing but rarely if ever harmful. They do not suck blood, and the itchiness is often caused by small scratches on the scalp from over enthusiastic combing or finger nails.

Causes
Social status means nothing to lice, but they do seem to be more commonly found on children's scalps as they make intimate contact more often than adults. Although lice cannot fly, jump or swim, they are expert climbers and will cling on to any passing hair. They have a natural camouflage and can be difficult to detect, especially when there are only a few small lice present. It is almost impossible to prevent them amongst young children.

Treatment and self care
You can detect them by using a fine steel or plastic comb (from your pharmacist) on wet hair. This is helped by using a conditioner. Unless you actually detect living, moving lice you do not need to treat. There are several treatment options:

- Hair lotions using insecticides. You need to also check all close family/friends by the 'wet combing' method and treat anyone who is found to have lice at the same time, to prevent re-infection. Ensure you have enough lotion to treat all those affected and follow the instructions on the packet carefully.
- The 'Bug Busting' treatment method. This depends solely on physically removing any lice present. Success depends largely upon adopting a painstaking approach – as described in the Bug Busting kit available from some pharmacies, and by mail order from Community Hygiene Concern (see *Contacts* on page 183).
- The electric comb. Battery-powered, this is run through the child's hair and electrocutes any lice in its path, but not the child. As with bug busting, success depends on the thoroughness of the approach.

Insecticide lotion is probably more effective than bug busting, but there is increasing resistance to the insecticides, both by the lice who are becoming immune to their effects and by the parents who fear that repeated use may have a harmful effect on the child's nervous system.

Whatever method of control is adopted, it is easier to use on short hair.

More information on the prevention and treatment of lice is available from the Department of Health (see *Contacts* on page 183)

H34155

Sun burn

Although there is some controversy over the danger of exposure to too much sunlight, we do know that it can be harmful. Over the past few decades there has been a dramatic increase in the number of cases of malignant melanoma, a particularly nasty and potentially lethal skin cancer. Once considered rare, it is still increasing possibly due to the desire for sun-drenched holidays. Australia has been in the forefront of educating people over the dangers of sunbathing.

Symptoms

Most people do not realise that they have badly burned themselves until later on in the day. The first sign of a burn is a reddening of the skin caused by blood vessels increasing in size to get rid of as much heat as possible. At this stage damage is already being done to the skin.

Causes

Ultra violet light (UV) can penetrate the outer layers of skin, especially in fair-skinned people. It heats and damages the lower layers causing skin loss. The body responds by increasing the amount of melanin, a black pigment, in the skin which prevents the sun from reaching the delicate lower skin layers.

Prevention

It's not too smart to be out in the sun wearing nothing but shorts, it's potentially deadly. Use a strong sun block (SPF 15 and over). Cover your child's body, especially the head, with appropriate clothing. Never leave a baby exposed to the sun, even if the weather is hazy.

Complications

If the exposure to the sun continues the skin will form blisters just as with a scald. These blisters burst very quickly and the covering skin is then lost exposing red skin beneath. If this is extensive, a large amount of body fluids can be lost; a particular danger to babies and small children who do not have a large body mass.

Like any burn, skin damaged by overexposure to UV can scar.

Long term exposure to the sun causes the collagen network within the skin to become less flexible. This makes the skin lose its elasticity so it droops, folds and wrinkles very easily.

Self care

A badly burnt baby or small child needs to go to hospital. Treat sun burn like any other burn. There are lotions you can apply which will ease the pain but they cannot prevent the damage which is already done. Give plenty of fluids and keep out of the sun for a few days. Use only tepid baths.

Note: There is no 'safe' exposure time. The rate at which you burn depends on the colour of your skin. Fair complexions are the easiest to damage with UV. Dark skin is the most resistant but will still be burned with prolonged exposure. Generally after 15 minutes on a first exposure white skin is already damaged.

Action

See your pharmacist.

Cuts and grazes

For a minor cut, press the wound with a clean fabric pad for a few minutes to help stop the bleeding. For a cut on an arm or leg, elevate the limb. Water may be used to wipe around the edge of the cut or graze. Once clean, apply a dressing such as a plaster.

Seek medical attention if:

- The cut is deep cut and the edges cannot be pulled together.
- Severe redness or swelling develops after a couple of days (this may be a sign of an infection).
- Severe bleeding from a wound needs immediate medical attention. While waiting for expert help, lie the child down and raise the injured part of the body above the level of the heart to help reduce blood loss. Place a clean cloth against the wound and press firmly. Secure this pad in place. Never use a tourniquet (something tied round the limb to stop the blood flow) - serious illness or even death can result from the blood clots which will form.

Burns and scalds

Any burn or scald requires immediate action.

Remove tight clothing if possible. Cool the affected area with cold water for at least 10 minutes, then cover with a light, non-fluffy material. For a limb, kitchen film or a polythene bag may be used. Don't burst any blisters and don't apply any cream or ointments. (The exception is mild sunburn, which may be soothed with a lotion like calamine.)

Seek medical attention if:
- The burn is larger than the size of the child's hand.
- The burn is on the face.
- The skin is broken.

Severe burns need urgent medical attention. Cool the burn down, cover it with a sterile dressing, and get the child to your local accident and emergency department immediately or call for an ambulance. While waiting for the ambulance, make them lie down and raise their legs. This helps keep blood available for the vital organs. Don't remove clothes if they are sticking to the skin.

Cradle cap

A harmless scale which builds up on the scalp.

Symptoms

A thick white/yellow waxy scale builds up on the scalp. There is no bleeding or obvious irritation unless too vigorous attempts are made to remove it. There is no fever and the child is perfectly well.

Causes

Like many other forms of eczema (see page 154), the cause is unknown.

Prevention

Routine cleaning will prevent it in most cases.

Complications

There are no serious complications.

Self care

A form of eczema, it responds well to simply rubbing the affected parts of the scalp with olive oil. Leave it on overnight before washing it off with a mild shampoo in the morning.

Shampoos are available from your pharmacist, but you should try rubbing with olive oil first. Ask your pharmacist for advice.

Cold sores (herpes simplex)

Cold sores are common, tend to recur and can be very sore.

Symptoms

The corners of the mouth are the mainly affected areas with crusty, oozing blisters.

Causes

Herpes is a virus which lies dormant in nerve endings within the skin. The virus erupts during stress, use of steroids and for vague reasons such as sunlight exposure. There is a well-recognised pattern:

- A tingling, itchy feeling is usually felt just before the rash forms.
- Tiny blisters appear, usually where the lips join the skin.
- The blisters become sore and itchy.
- They then crust over and last about one week before disappearing.

Prevention and treatment

Herpes is highly infectious and can be passed on through kissing particularly while blisters are erupting. Babies tend to get kissed a great deal, so they are at risk of picking up a herpes simplex infection. People are at most risk of passing on an infection while the blisters are erupting so they should avoid kissing the baby during this time.

Paracetamol elixir helps with the pain, but for babies under 3 months use only under strict advice from your pharmacist or GP.

Lip salves can be applied before taking the baby into bright sunlight. The baby should also wear a hat.

There are topical medicines which limit the infection (ask your pharmacist).

Heat rash

All babies and children will have a rash at some time and these may sometimes be simply a 'heat rash'

Symptoms

It often looks like a fine pattern of tiny red spots which come and go but tend to disappear if their temperature is lowered.

The child will be perfectly well with no other symptoms. A meningitis rash will not blanch when pressed with the side of a glass tumbler (see *Meningitis* on page 174).

Causes

A cold or other viral infection is the most common cause. Too many clothes or bedding will also cause it.

Prevention

If your child gets too hot cool them down immediately by removing their clothes and keeping them in a cool room with tepid sponging. Keep an open mind, if things are getting worse call your doctor/999/112 (see *Rashes* on pages 162 to 164 and *Fever* on page 177).

Hives (urticaria)

Hives (urticaria or nettle rash) are small raised red spots, often itchy, which you can feel. They are rarely serious unless combined with any breathing problems. The rash will usually disappear in a few hours without any treatment.

Causes

It is most often caused by a viral infection but may be caused by certain foods and plants (eg, nettles).

Complications

Rarely the rash is severe and associated with breathing difficulties. This is an emergency so dial 999/112.

Treatment and care

Antihistamine creams and anti-histamine medicine may help. Ask your pharmacist.

If there is any shortness of breath dial 999/112.

Purpura

Serious problems are rare but these irregularly-shaped dark red spots could follow an allergic reaction to infection or some disorder of the blood.

Symptoms

The spots are not usually irritating, range from around pin-head size to a couple of centimetres (around one inch), tend to come and go and will not turn white (blanch) when pressed with a glass tumbler.

Causes

Children between 2 and 10 years are most likely to be affected. There are a number of causes, but anything that affects the ability of the blood to clot can cause this rash.

Treatment

Dial 999/112.

Nappy rash

Rashes in the nappy area are common but are not inevitable and can be reduced in severity or avoided completely.

Symptoms

The rash is usually red, not raised and confined to the nappy area.

Causes

Urine is highly irritant, especially in babies, as it contains ammonia. If it is cleaned away quickly enough, or the baby is allowed to have the nappy off for a while, the rash will not appear.

Prevention

As far as is possible, change each nappy immediately following soiling. Remember that urine can be every bit as irritating as faeces. Avoid disposable wipes containing alcohol (remember aftershaves after a bad shave? Same thing but on a far more sensitive surface than your chin) or moisturising chemicals. Instead use plenty of warm water. Leave the nappy off as much as is practical, particularly any plastic pants. Dry, cool skin rarely forms a nappy rash. Re-usable nappies should be washed as directed by the manufacturer. Avoid caustic household detergents which tend to leave residual traces no matter how well they are rinsed.

Complications

An angry red rash which does not respond or extends beyond the nappy area may be a fungal infection (candida). You need an anti-fungal cream and possibly an oral anti-fungal agent as it often starts in the mouth. Ask your pharmacist or doctor.

Self care

Promptly treat any rash appearing with ointment from your pharmacist.

Avoid talcum powder. It can cake badly and cause even more irritation.

Scabies

Although intensely itchy, scabies is rarely a serious condition.

Symptoms
Red lines which follow the burrows of the mite as it travels in the skin soon merge with the inevitable scratching. It is usually worse at night when the mite is most active.

Causes
Scabies is caused by a mite which burrows just under the skin, often between the fingers, on wrists, elbows and the genital areas causing a red rash. It can only come from contact with infected people.

Prevention
It is very difficult to prevent.

Complications
Bacterial infection from excessive scratching can make the situation worse.

Treatment and self care
Use lotions or creams which are available from your pharmacist over the counter or on prescription. All of the body will need to be covered with the ointment for 24 hours and all clothing and bedding should be washed thoroughly. All the family must also be treated. Use under strict advice from doctor or pharmacist.

'Slapped cheek' disease

Few conditions fit the name better. This is a mild illness characterised by a very vivid, red fiery rash on the cheeks, and a less intense rash on the arms and legs with occasional joint pains. It is also known as 'slapped cheek syndrome' and 'fifth disease'.

Cause
Despite the popular name (the formal name is erythema infectiosum), it is not caused by abuse but by infection with a virus called Human Parvovirus B19.

Treatment and self care
Generally it is self-limiting and will disappear on its own but you can make life more pleasant for the child with some simple treatments:

- Sponge the baby with tepid water, all over. By allowing body heat to dry the skin rather than towelling it dry the child will cool down quickly and feel much better.
- Sugar-free paracetamol syrup helps to help reduce fever and eases aches and pains. Take careful note of the dose on the bottle.
- Don't put too many clothes on them. No clothes at all in a warm room is best.
- Keep the fluids up, they will lose water through a fever.

Infant rashes

Is the rash a crusty white scale on the scalp?

YES → *See* **Cradle cap**
ADVICE Cradle cap is a form of eczema, it responds well to simply rubbing the affected parts of the scalp with olive oil. Leave it on over night before washing it off with a mild shampoo in the morning. **See your pharmacist.**

NO

Is there a fever (the temperature is over 38°C/100.4°F)?

YES → *See* **Rashes with fever**

NO

Is the rash mainly in the nappy area?

YES → *See* **Nappy rash**
ADVICE Rashes in the nappy area are common but can be reduced in severity or avoided completely.
- As far as possible, change each nappy following soiling.
- As much as possible, leave the nappy off, particularly any plastic pants. Dry cool skin rarely forms a nappy rash.
- An angry red rash which won't respond or extends beyond the nappy area may be a fungal infection (Candida). **Ask your pharmacist or doctor.**

NO

Is the rash red, itchy, flaky and in more than one place?

YES → *See* **Eczema**
ADVICE Eczema covers a range of skin problems. There is a wide range of products which will help stop the itchiness and keep the skin moist. Follow your doctor's advice on the use of topical steroid creams. Call NHS Direct, **but call your doctor if:**
- The eczema is spreading very quickly.
- The skin is becoming infected.
- There is severe pain.

NO

Is the rash blotchy red and difficult to feel?

YES → *See* **Heat rash**
ADVICE All babies and children will have a heat rash at some time. No treatment is required other than lowering their temperature by moving them from the heat, removing their clothes and keeping them in a cool room.

NO

Is the rash dark red, mainly on the elbows, legs, buttocks and does it change its appearance and place on the skin?

YES → *See* **Purpura**
ADVICE Serious problems are rare but these irregularly shaped dark red spots could follow an allergic reaction to infection or some disorder of the blood. **Stop answering the questions and call NHS Direct.**

NO

Self care advice
- A rash alone is unlikely to be serious.
- Encourage the child to rest and observe closely for signs of illness.
- Ensure the child is drinking plenty of fluids.
- Paracetamol may be helpful if the child is restless.
- Antihistamine cream may provide some relief - a pharmacist will be able to advise you further.
- Calamine lotion will give relief for a short time.
- 2 tablespoons of sodium bicarbonate added to bath water may relieve any itching.
- If the condition gets worse or if any other symptoms develop **call NHS Direct.**

Itchy rashes

Is the rash **red, smooth and slightly raised (you can feel it)?**

YES → See **Hives & Urticaria**
ADVICE Hives can be a reaction to food (e.g. shell fish, strawberries), medicines, plants (e.g. nettles) or a viral infection. The rash will usually disappear in a few hours without any treatment. Call NHS Direct if the rash has not disappeared after 24 hours. **Dial 999/112 if there are any breathing difficulties or they cannot swallow.**

NO ↓

Is the rash only at the **lips and mouth corners?**

YES → See **Cold sores**
ADVICE It could be a cold sore.
- Once infected avoid sudden changes in temperature and sun exposure.
- Use simple painkillers such as paracetamol (not aspirin in children under 12 years).
- Use a lip salve before going into bright sunlight.
- Aciclovir cream from your pharmacist will limit the outbreak.

NO ↓

Is the rash **ring shaped with red scales?**

YES → **ADVICE** Ringworm (Tinea) can affect many parts of the body particularly the groin and scalp. Keep the area well ventilated and dry. Use an antifungal cream or shampoo available from your pharmacist and keep the baby's face cloth and towel separate. **Ringworm is infectious.**

NO ↓

Is the rash **itchy, on the fingers, hand or wrist?**

YES → See **Scabies**
ADVICE Scabies is caused by a mite which burrows just under the skin, often between the fingers, wrists, elbows and the genital areas. Ointments are available from your pharmacist. All of the body will need to be covered with the ointment for 24 hours and all clothing and bedding should be washed thoroughly.

NO ↓

Is it **raised with one or more in the same area?**

YES → See **Insect bite**
ADVICE At first insect bites can be mistaken for more serious things. If you look very closely you can generally see the small hole of the actual bite. **See your pharmacist.**

NO ↓

Self care advice
- A rash alone is unlikely to be serious.
- Encourage the child to rest and watch closely for signs of illness.
- Ensure the child is drinking plenty of fluids.
- Paracetamol may be helpful if the child is restless.
- Antihistamine cream may provide some relief - a pharmacist will be able to advise you further.
- Calamine lotion will give relief for a short time.
- 2 tablespoons of sodium bicarbonate added to bath water may relieve any itching.
- If the condition gets worse or if any other symptoms develop **call NHS Direct.**

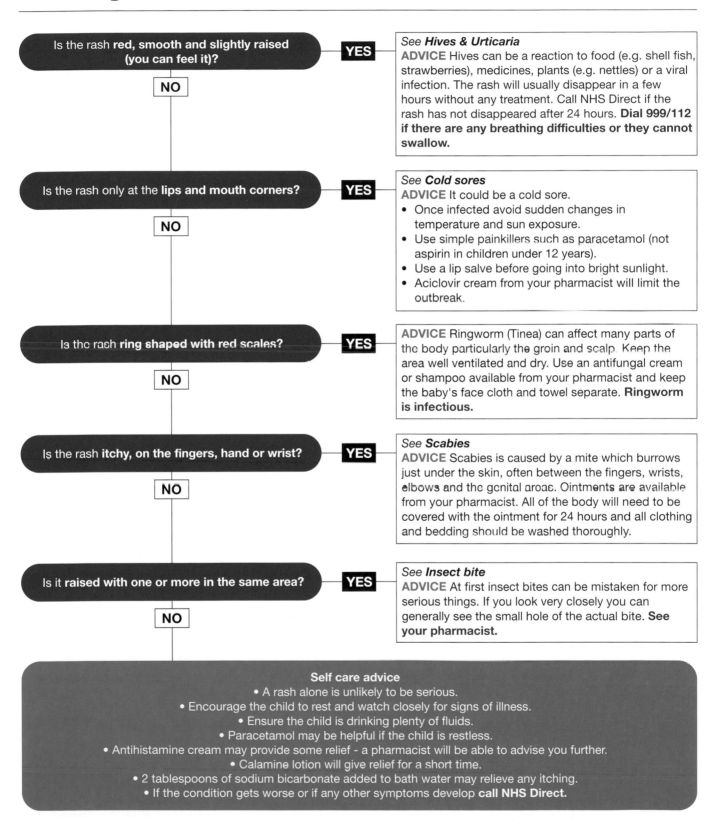

Rashes with fever

Is the rash **purple and does not turn white when pressed with a tumbler?** — **YES**

See *Meningitis*
ADVICE **Dial 999/112.**

NO

Are the spots **red, difficult to feel;** are the **eyes sore,** is there **a cough** or **a runny nose?** — **YES**

See *Measles*
ADVICE Rashes in children are common.
- Use paracetamol elixir for fever and/or aches and pains.
- Cough medicines are of little value but do ease ticklish throats. Place a bowl of water in the room to the increase humidity.
- Avoid dehydration. Feverish small children rapidly lose water. It also makes a tickly cough worse.

NO

Are there **swellings on the neck?** — **YES**

See *Rubella*
ADVICE It could be german measles (rubella). Now uncommon thanks to the MMR vaccine. The real danger comes later in life if an unvaccinated woman becomes infected with german measles (rubella) while pregnant. For this major reason alone both boys and girls should be immunised with this very safe vaccine.

NO

If you can feel the spot are they turning into **small blisters?** — **YES**

See *Chicken pox*
ADVICE It could be chicken pox. Intensely itchy, tiny clear blisters soon follow. Fresh red spots are usually seen next to blisters and crusts.
- Most children are free from chicken pox in less than two weeks.
- Dab calamine lotion on the infected spots which should ease the itching.
- Use cool baths without soap every three to four hours for the first couple of days. Add a few tablespoons of sodium bicarbonate to the bath water.
- Antihistamines are available from your pharmacist. These help reduce itching and promote sleep, so use them just before bed time.
- Paracetamol helps reduce the fever.

NO

Self care advice
- A rash alone is unlikely to be serious.
- Encourage the child to rest and observe closely for signs of illness.
- Ensure the child is drinking plenty of fluids.
- Paracetamol may be helpful if the child is restless.
- Antihistamine cream may provide some relief - a pharmacist will be able to advise you further.
- Calamine lotion will give relief for a short time.
- 2 tablespoons of sodium bicarbonate added to bath water may relieve any itching.
- If the condition gets worse or if any other symptoms develop **call NHS Direct.**

PART ⑨ Bones and joints

Broken bones and dislocations

Broken bones and dislocations always need immediate medical attention. They can be very painful, and you can help by reassuring the child and keeping them still.

Broken limbs

Steady and support the limb with your hands. If a leg is broken, place padding around it to prevent movement. A broken arm or collar bone should be supported on the affected side to the body.

Injured neck or spine

Keep the injured child as still as possible without heavily restraining them. It is essential not to move someone with a neck or spine injury unless they are in imminent danger of further injury. If the casualty becomes unconscious, carefully place them in recovery position while keeping the spine in line at all times.

Dislocated joints

Never try to force a joint back into place. Simply support the limb and seek emergency help

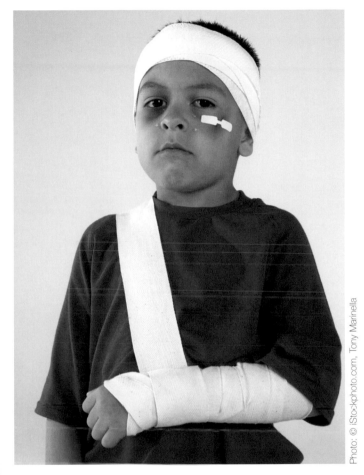

Photo: © iStockphoto.com, Tony Marinella

Sprains, strains and bruising

Remember 'RICE' (Rest, Ice, Compress, Elevation).
*   Rest the injured part as much as possible.
*   Immediately after the injury, pack the area with ice wrapped in a cloth – a bag of frozen peas works well – to reduce swelling. Keep the ice in place for about 10 minutes.
*   Gently compress the injury and bind the area with an elastic bandage so it is well supported, but make sure you doesn't restrict blood flow.
*   To minimise swelling, keep the injured part elevated as much of the time as possible.
    Seek medical attention if:
*   You think there may be a broken bone – immobilise the area with padding and seek aid immediately.
*   Symptoms don't improve.
*   Bruising remains after several days.

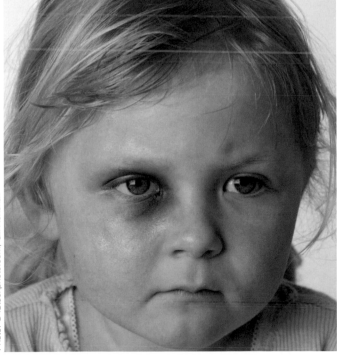

Photo: © iStockphoto.com, Gill Henshall

PART  **Head**

Nose bleeds

Nose bleeds are common and most are easily dealt with. Sit the child down, leaning slightly forward, and tell them to breathe through the mouth. Then pinch the nose firmly for about 10 minutes. Seek medical help if the bleeding continues for more than 30 minutes or if you suspect the nose is broken.

Oral thrush

Contrary to common thought, thrush is not caused by bacteria or viruses. It is candida albicans, a yeast fungus, which causes the problem. For some reason it is most common young children and babies, even though there is often no apparent reason for it to grow. It can also be encouraged by repeated courses of antibiotics or steroids.

Symptoms

Sore, creamy yellow patches on the inner cheeks and throat. These turn into a nasty raw looking area when rubbed. Babies can have difficulty feeding and may cry, particularly if drinking fruit juice.

Causes

Oral thrush is very common in babies and there is often no obvious cause, other than (if applicable) repeated antibiotic or steroid treatments.

Prevention

Although bottle feeding is not a direct cause provided the equipment is properly sterilised, breastfeeding may give a degree of protection from infections generally.

Treatment

A course of antifungal drops will generally clear the infection quickly, but it can recur. If it does, you should seek medical advice.

Sticky eye

A sticky eye which is also red is likely to be conjunctivitis caused by a bacterial or viral infection that affects the lining of the outer membrane of the eye and the lids. It commonly affects both eyes at the same time.

Treatment and self care

- Gently bathe the affected eye with clean cotton wool soaked in cooled, tepid, boiled water.
- Throw away the cotton wool after each wipe.
- Wipe from the inner eyelid outwards.
- Do not share towels or flannels with other members of the family as conjunctivitis can be very infectious.
- Make an appointment to see your doctor if both eyes are infected or they don't clear up in a few days.

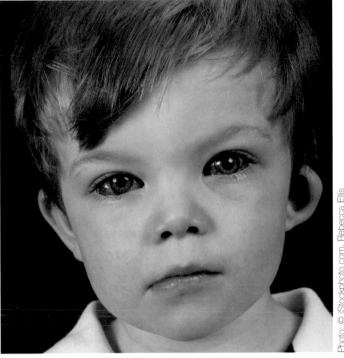

Photo: © iStockphoto.com, Rebecca Ellis

Blood in the white of the eye (subconjunctival haemorrhage)

A thin transparent layer covers the white of the eye called the conjunctiva. Bright red blood over the conjunctiva can be quite alarming yet it is generally completely harmless and very common, and parents worry unnecessarily that the child may have been hit or dropped. Tiny blood vessels beneath the protective layer (conjunctiva) burst and a small amount of blood is trapped under the conjunctiva.

Symptoms

The blood appears very quickly. Generally the blood will be over one part of the white of the eye but sometimes may cover most or all of it. The conjunctiva is tethered down in a ring around the transparent very front of the eye, the cornea. Blood can travel freely under the conjunctiva but not over the cornea itself.

Causes

It is common in babies and children when they cry for long periods.

Complications

Within a week or so it should disappear altogether.

Action

Unless there was trauma involved there is no need for a medical examination as the blood will gradually disperse on its own.

Blocked tear ducts

Even without crying there is always tear fluid running on to the surface of the eye to provide oxygen and nutrients, as the very front of the eye (the cornea) has no blood vessels. Watery eyes can therefore be caused by this tear fluid failing to drain away through the tear ducts at the nose side of each eye (this is why your nose 'runs' when you cry hard). Blocked tear ducts which have yet to open properly are a common cause, but a bacterial or viral infection (see *Sticky eye* on page 167) can also be a cause and is usually accompanied by a sticky discharge and redness around the eyes.

Treatment

If it is not settling, or there is also a 'sticky eye' or red eye, ask your doctor's advice.

Your health visitor can show you how to massage the area gently to help clear any blockage.

Always bathe the eye from the nose side outwards, using a fresh clean piece of cotton wool soaked in cooled boiled water each time. Do not use the same bit twice. Wash your hands before and afterwards and use a separate towel or flannel if there is any sign of infection, as it is highly contagious.

Cleft lip and palate

Times change. Cleft lip and palate were once the subject of myth, fear and abuse. Not only are abnormalities infinitely more acceptable in modern society, we now have the ability to treat them often very successfully. Just as well, as about one child in 1000 will be affected, not common but then not very rare either. The upper lip may have a defect which may be no more than a small notch, or which may extend right up to join one nostril. A gap in the roof of the mouth, cleft palate, may partially or completely divide it. Sometimes there are two gaps in the upper lip, extending up to both nostrils, and these may be associated with partial or complete cleft palate. Alternatively there may be only a cleft palate on its own, without any lip defect.

Symptoms

Unlike some congenital abnormalities, such as those affecting the heart, a cleft lip is often obvious. This is actually an advantage as it can then be recognised and steps taken early to rectify the situation. Feeding problems can often arise but in most cases these can be overcome with either bottle feeding or breastfeeding with a nipple shield which seals the area around the nipple, allowing the baby to suckle.

Causes

Facial development in the womb is incredibly complex with various parts needing to fuse along the mid-line. Any failure to join properly can cause a cleft lip or palate. Myths surround the whole area of cleft lip, most designed to make the parent feel as guilty and dreadful as possible. In truth we don't know the underlying cause although it may be possible to reduce the risk.

Diagnosis

Generally it is the parent, often the mother, who realises there is a problem. Sometimes a cleft palate will go unnoticed for longer until feeding becomes a problem. Referral to a surgeon specialising in this area will establish the extent of the problem and all children will benefit from modern surgery.

Prevention

There is no definitive way of prevention but it makes sense to follow guidelines on vitamin supplements, avoiding drugs, tobacco and alcohol during pregnancy.

Complications

Feeding is not a serious problem in almost all cases, but speech development can be affected unless early intervention takes place. This has major implications for the child's education. It's worth saying it again that modern surgery really can and does make a major change in the situation so there is no need for despondency.

Treatment

The surgical management of these conditions has improved greatly in recent decades and it is now rare to see the obvious deformity, called 'hare lip', resulting from treatment of a cleft lip. Good surgical repair is possible, usually between three months and one year of age.

Treatment of cleft palate begins immediately after birth. A small device called a palatal obturator is used to cover the opening to help the baby to feed. There is often a team involved which includes surgeons, speech therapists, physiotherapists and dentists.

Earache

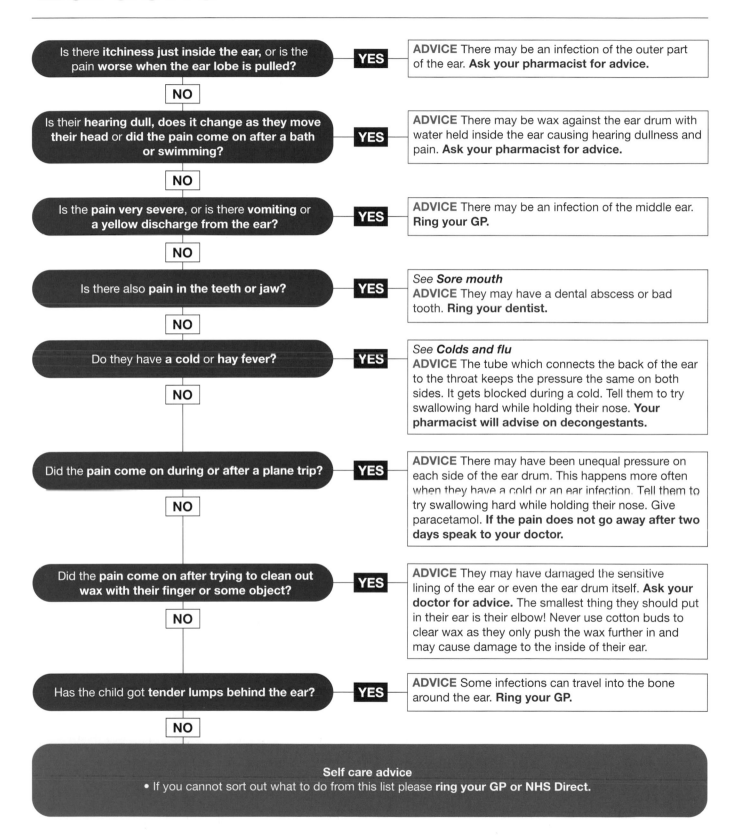

Is there itchiness just inside the ear, or is the pain **worse when the ear lobe is pulled?**

YES → **ADVICE** There may be an infection of the outer part of the ear. **Ask your pharmacist for advice.**

NO

Is their hearing dull, does it change as they move their head or **did the pain come on after a bath or swimming?**

YES → **ADVICE** There may be wax against the ear drum with water held inside the ear causing hearing dullness and pain. **Ask your pharmacist for advice.**

NO

Is the pain very severe, or is there **vomiting** or **a yellow discharge from the ear?**

YES → **ADVICE** There may be an infection of the middle ear. **Ring your GP.**

NO

Is there also pain in the teeth or jaw?

YES → See **Sore mouth**
ADVICE They may have a dental abscess or bad tooth. **Ring your dentist.**

NO

Do they have a cold or hay fever?

YES → See **Colds and flu**
ADVICE The tube which connects the back of the ear to the throat keeps the pressure the same on both sides. It gets blocked during a cold. Tell them to try swallowing hard while holding their nose. **Your pharmacist will advise on decongestants.**

NO

Did the pain come on during or after a plane trip?

YES → **ADVICE** There may have been unequal pressure on each side of the ear drum. This happens more often when they have a cold or an ear infection. Tell them to try swallowing hard while holding their nose. Give paracetamol. **If the pain does not go away after two days speak to your doctor.**

NO

Did the pain come on after trying to clean out wax with their finger or some object?

YES → **ADVICE** They may have damaged the sensitive lining of the ear or even the ear drum itself. **Ask your doctor for advice.** The smallest thing they should put in their ear is their elbow! Never use cotton buds to clear wax as they only push the wax further in and may cause damage to the inside of their ear.

NO

Has the child got tender lumps behind the ear?

YES → **ADVICE** Some infections can travel into the bone around the ear. **Ring your GP.**

NO

Self care advice
• If you cannot sort out what to do from this list please **ring your GP or NHS Direct.**

Head injury

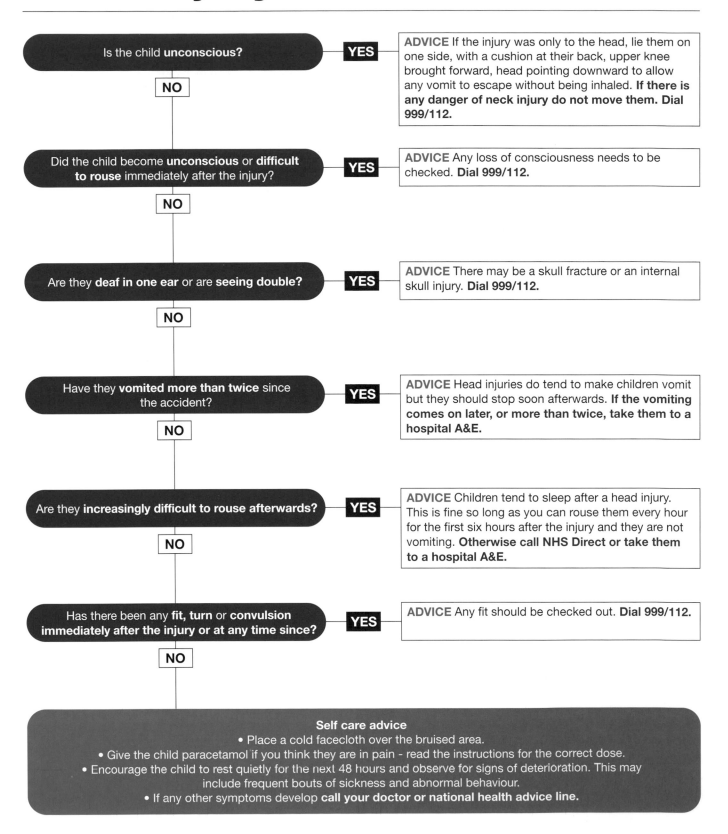

Is the child unconscious?

YES → **ADVICE** If the injury was only to the head, lie them on one side, with a cushion at their back, upper knee brought forward, head pointing downward to allow any vomit to escape without being inhaled. **If there is any danger of neck injury do not move them. Dial 999/112.**

NO ↓

Did the child become unconscious or difficult to rouse immediately after the injury?

YES → **ADVICE** Any loss of consciousness needs to be checked. **Dial 999/112.**

NO ↓

Are they deaf in one ear or are seeing double?

YES → **ADVICE** There may be a skull fracture or an internal skull injury. **Dial 999/112.**

NO ↓

Have they vomited more than twice since the accident?

YES → **ADVICE** Head injuries do tend to make children vomit but they should stop soon afterwards. **If the vomiting comes on later, or more than twice, take them to a hospital A&E.**

NO ↓

Are they increasingly difficult to rouse afterwards?

YES → **ADVICE** Children tend to sleep after a head injury. This is fine so long as you can rouse them every hour for the first six hours after the injury and they are not vomiting. **Otherwise call NHS Direct or take them to a hospital A&E.**

NO ↓

Has there been any fit, turn or convulsion immediately after the injury or at any time since?

YES → **ADVICE** Any fit should be checked out. **Dial 999/112.**

NO ↓

Self care advice
- Place a cold facecloth over the bruised area.
- Give the child paracetamol if you think they are in pain - read the instructions for the correct dose.
- Encourage the child to rest quietly for the next 48 hours and observe for signs of deterioration. This may include frequent bouts of sickness and abnormal behaviour.
- If any other symptoms develop **call your doctor or national health advice line.**

Sore mouth

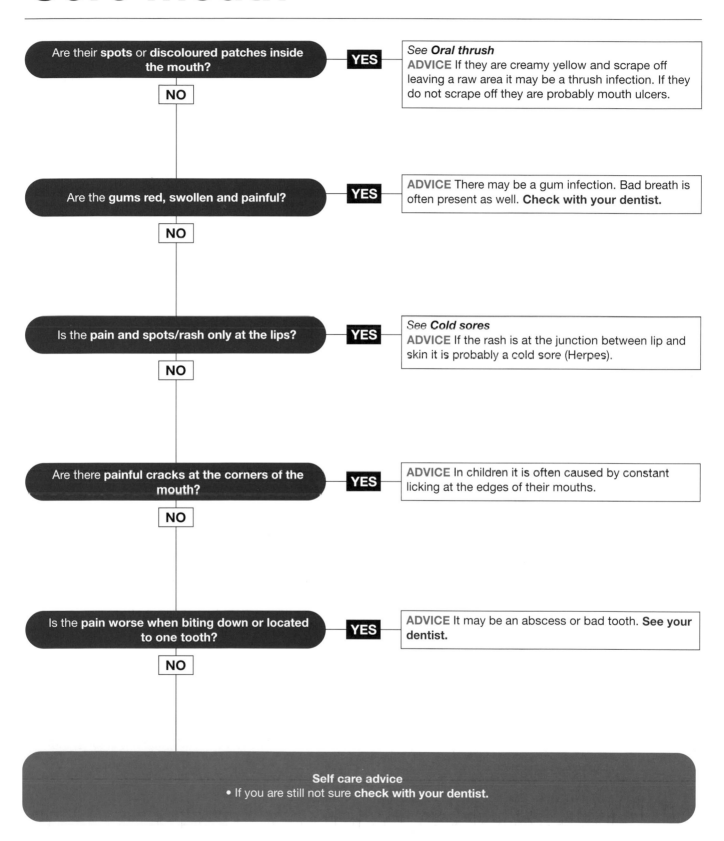

Are their **spots** or **discoloured patches inside the mouth?** — **YES**

See *Oral thrush*
ADVICE If they are creamy yellow and scrape off leaving a raw area it may be a thrush infection. If they do not scrape off they are probably mouth ulcers.

NO

Are the **gums red, swollen and painful?** — **YES**

ADVICE There may be a gum infection. Bad breath is often present as well. **Check with your dentist.**

NO

Is the **pain and spots/rash only at the lips?** — **YES**

See *Cold sores*
ADVICE If the rash is at the junction between lip and skin it is probably a cold sore (Herpes).

NO

Are there **painful cracks at the corners of the mouth?** — **YES**

ADVICE In children it is often caused by constant licking at the edges of their mouths.

NO

Is the **pain worse when biting down or located to one tooth?** — **YES**

ADVICE It may be an abscess or bad tooth. **See your dentist.**

NO

Self care advice
• If you are still not sure **check with your dentist.**

PART 9 Infectious diseases

Chicken pox

The incubation period (the time from contact with the virus and onset of symptoms) is between 7 to 21 days. In most cases there are no symptoms before the rash appears. It is one of the more harmless infections.

Symptoms

A mild fever, stomach ache and a general feeling of being unwell can occur a day or two before the flat, red rash appears. This generally begins on the scalp, face and back, but can spread to any body surface although it is rarely seen on the palms of the hands or soles of the feet.

- Intensely itchy, tiny clear blisters full of virus particles then appear.
- New blisters appear as fresh red spots, usually seen next to old blisters and crusts.
- It generally takes less than two weeks to clear.

Causes

Chicken pox is a highly infectious virus and spreads quickly, especially between children. Close contact is all that is required to pass on the infection.

Prevention

There is no vaccine licensed in this country at present. Some parents advocate 'pox parties' to get the child infected at an early age. This is probably not wise, as there is no guarantee of infection in later life.

Complications

Thankfully, complications are very rare in children. There are reported cases of encephalitis (inflammation of the brain), meningitis or pneumonia but they are extremely rare.

More serious complications are seen in children who are taking medicines such as steroids as they can lower the body's immune defence system, or who have a medical condition which lowers their natural resistance.

Self care

- A few teaspoons of sodium bicarbonate in a cool bath can help relieve the itch.
- There are products available from your pharmacist to provide temporary relief.
- Calamine lotion is a traditional treatment to stop the itching. Put some in a spray bottle (as used on plants) and spray the child whilst stood in the bath or shower. The droplets so created cool the blisters and soothe quickly.
- Cotton socks on inquisitive hands will prevent too much scratching which can lead to infection.
- Paracetamol elixir helps reduce the fever. Do not give aspirin to children under 16 years of age.
- Ice lollies help lower temperature, provide sugar and water and at the same time reduce the irritation of mouth infection. They may be used in children over 4 years old.

More information

Chicken pox is no longer infectious 5 days after the blisters first appear or when all the blisters have scabbed over, whichever comes first.

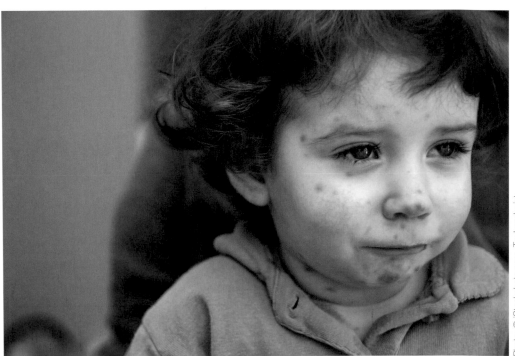

Photo: © iStockphoto.com, Tor Lindqvist

Measles

Young children are most vulnerable to this highly contagious viral infection. The 'triple vaccine' MMR (mumps, measles, rubella) vaccination programme made measles very rare in the UK, but it has now made an unwelcome return as vaccination rates have fallen in response to fears amongst parents over highly-publicised but un-substantiated links with autism and Crohn's disease.

Symptoms

There is generally a pattern which is easy to recognise:
- Red eyes and sensitivity to light.
- Tiredness and general fatigue.
- Loss of appetite.
- Running nose and sneezing.
- A temperature of around 39°C (102.2°F).
- Irritable dry cough.
- Tiny white spots in the mouth and throat.
- A blotchy red rash that starts behind the ears, spreads to the face and then to the rest of the body and lasts for up to seven days.

Transmission

There is an incubation period (the time the disease takes to show after initial infection) of around 10 to 12 days. Physical contact, sneezing and clothing contaminated with nasal secretions all help to spread the infection.

Prevention

Vaccination is the best way but once a child has had measles they are also immune.

Complications

There are rare but serious complications from measles such as meningitis and pneumonia. More commonly, eyes and ears develop secondary infection which may need antibiotic treatment.

Treatment and self care

There is no cure for measles so once the rash starts it is a matter of treating the symptoms.
- Use a ball of damp cotton wool to clean away any crustiness around the eyes.
- Draw the curtains or blinds to ease their eyes from bright sunlight.
- Although cough medicines are of little proven value they may ease ticklish throats, but also try placing a bowl of water in the room.
- High temperature, aches and pains can be treated with paracetamol elixir.
- Feverish small children dehydrate very quickly which can make their cough worse. Keep up their fluids.

Ideally, you should keep your child away from others for at least 7 days after the start of the rash, easier said than done.

After four days the child usually feels better.

Colds and flu

Most of us can't tell the difference between a bad cold and flu, so you will be delighted to hear that most doctors can't either. The problem with children is they look so awful when it is just a bad cold. Even so, there are easy and effective ways to treat your child's colds and flu symptoms at home and with medicines from your pharmacy.

How to treat cold and flu symptoms:
- Get them to drink plenty of fluids.
- Use paracetamol (Calpol) according to the instructions (don't give aspirin to a child under 16 years because of the danger of its link with Reye's Syndrome). This will ease their sore throat and muscle aches while bringing their temperature down. Always take the suggested dosage for all medications.
- Don't encourage strenuous exercise, but at the same time it is often better if they sit up and watch TV rather than overheating in a bed. You can also keep a better eye on them.
- Encourage them to cover their mouth when they cough and sneeze.
- Wash your hands regularly as the virus is passed through skin contact.
- Keep the bedroom well-ventilated.
- If they do have flu let them take it easy.

You should contact your GP or ring NHS Direct (0845 46 47) if they are experiencing severe or prolonged symptoms, shortness of breath or are coughing up blood or phlegm (see *Fever* on page 177).

Photo: © iStockphoto.com, Suzanne Tucker

Antibiotics

Some people expect their GP to always give antibiotics to treat children's colds and flu symptoms. Colds and flu are viral illnesses. Antibiotics do not work on viral illness and in fact they can do more harm than good.

Meningitis/septicaemia

Although a rare illness, this causes an inflammation of the brain lining which can be fatal, so it is rightly seen as a real threat by parents. Unfortunately the symptoms can be easily be mistaken for flu or a bad cold. Worse still, it is more difficult to be certain with babies and young children. If you are not sure, you must call your doctor/999/112.

Hib immunisation has reduced the number of people suffering from some types of meningitis/septicaemia. Unfortunately, we do not have vaccines for every type of meningitis/septicaemia, so we all still need to watch out for the symptoms.

Symptoms

Babies under 2 years may show:
- A difficulty to wake.
- A cry which may be high-pitched and different from normal.
- Vomiting repeatedly, not just after feeds.
- Refusing feeds, either from the bottle, breast or by spoon.
- Skin which may appear pale or blotchy, possibly with a red/purple rash which does not fade when you press a tumbler glass or a finger against the rash.
- The soft spot on top of your baby's head (the fontanelle) may be tight or bulging.
- The baby may seem irritable and dislike being handled.
- The body may be floppy or else stiff with jerky movements.

Remember, a fever may not be present in the early stages, and the symptoms can appear in any order. Not all babies show all of these signs.

Causes

Meningitis can be caused by either bacteria or viruses; in most cases bacterial causes are more serious.

Prevention

Vaccination for meningitis C for children and young people up to 17 years of age is safe and extremely effective. Some forms of meningitis do not, as yet, have a vaccination so the disease can still occur. It pays to keep an open mind when faced with puzzling signs of infection. Always call your GP/999/112 if you are concerned that things are not getting better.

People who have been in contact with someone who has had meningitis should contact a close relative of the patient to find out any instructions that they may have been given. Otherwise your doctor will be able to give you appropriate advice. Only those who have been in very close contact with the infected person (referred to as 'kissing contacts') are given antibiotics and vaccination.

Pneumococcal disease

Invasive pneumococcal infections occur from *Streptococcus Pneumoniae* a bacterium causing meningitis, septicaemia (blood poisoning) and serious pneumonia. The bacterium can also cause less serious, but more common infections such as otitis media (middle ear infection), sinusitis and various chest infections.

Pneumococcal meningitis

Although viral meningitis is more common, pneumococcal meningitis (infection of the covering of the brain or spinal cord) is the UK's second most common form of bacterial meningitis and is amongst the most deadly in toddlers (see *Meningitis* on page 174).

Toddlers may experience:
- A severe headache.
- Stiff neck.
- Aversion to bright lights.
- Fever.
- Vomiting.

Approximately one in five children who contract pneumococcal meningitis will die, and 50% of survivors will be left with permanent disabilities, including deafness, blindness or cerebral palsy.

Invasive pneumococcal pneumonia

The pneumococcus bacteria is the most common cause of bacterial pneumonia. Classic bacterial pneumonia (infection of the lungs) starts suddenly with shivering fits, fever, pains in the chest and coughing.

The cough is dry at first, but within days the toddler starts to cough up phlegm. The phlegm is usually yellow or bloodstained. Breathing is typically fast and shallow. The infected toddler may gasp for air and may even go bluish around the lips and nails due to the lack of air. It hurts to breathe in deeply or cough.

Approximately 1 in 200 children in the UK are admitted to hospital before the age of five as a result of pneumococcal pneumonia, the commonest bacterial form of pneumonia in children under the age of two.

Pneumococcal blood poisoning (septicaemia)

Blood poisoning (septicaemia) usually begins with fever and chills. Excessive sweating may occur. The heart rate and respiratory rate rise in association with high fever. The affected toddler will feel very ill with profound feelings of weakness.

As the condition evolves they may begin to feel very cold and clammy. The skin becomes very pale and there may be tiny spots on the skin, which do not blanch when a glass tumbler is applied to the skin over the spot.

Prevention

A vaccine (see *Immunisation* on page 20) will usually be given as three doses, at two, four and thirteen months of age. Each dose will be given on a separate occasion. There is also a catch-up pneumococcal vaccination programme for all infants and young children under the age of 2 years, the age group at greatest risk.

German measles (rubella)

This once common and highly infections condition is now uncommon thanks to the MMR vaccine. Even so, with the confusion over the triple vaccine (MMR) the number of childhood cases is steadily rising.

Symptoms

The child is rarely ill but will have a mildly raised temperature and swollen glands on the neck and base of the skull.

The pin-head sized flat, red spots last around two days and need no treatment other than possibly some paracetamol for the slight fever.

Causes

The virus is very contagious and will spread quickly in a population which is not immune.

Prevention

Vaccination for girls and boys is both safe and effective.

Complications

Very rarely the virus that causes German measles (rubella) will cause an inflammation of the brain (encephalitis).

The real danger comes in later life if an unvaccinated woman becomes infected with German measles (rubella) while pregnant. For this major reason alone both boys and girls should be immunised.

Treatment and self care

Paracetamol will reduce the mild fever.

Roseola

This common condition is also known as 'fourth disease' and 'three-day fever'. It is more common in babies under one year old. Generally it shows itself with a high fever which lasts for around three or four days. As the fever drops, a rose-coloured, fine, flat, red spotty rash appears on the trunk. This spreads and then fades within 24 hours. Measles may first come to mind, but unlike measles the rash appears on the trunk first.

Treatment and self care

There is no 'cure', but it is almost always a mild condition which needs only simple care as for any fever:

● Sponge the child with tepid water, all over. Allow the body heat to dry the skin rather than towelling it dry as it takes off the body heat as the water evaporates. This can be repeated as often as necessary.
● Regular doses of sugar-free paracetamol syrup help reduce fever and combat aches and pains, but take great care to use according to the manufacturer's instructions. If you are not sure, ask your pharmacist.
● Take their clothes off. In a warm room the child needs only a tee shirt.
● Keep up with the fluids.

Fever

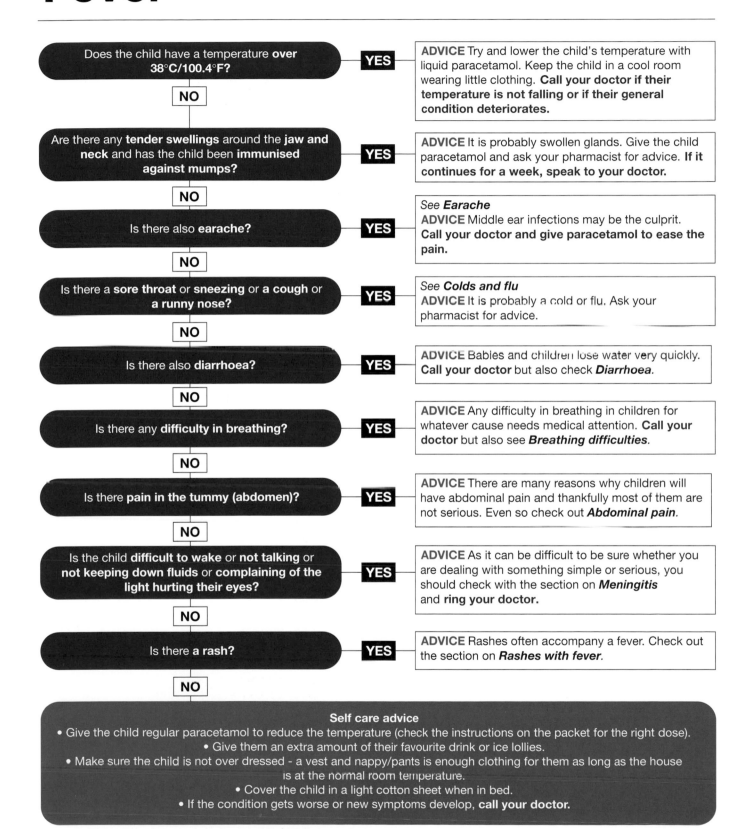

Does the child have a temperature **over 38°C/100.4°F?**

YES — **ADVICE** Try and lower the child's temperature with liquid paracetamol. Keep the child in a cool room wearing little clothing. **Call your doctor if their temperature is not falling or if their general condition deteriorates.**

NO

Are there any **tender swellings** around the **jaw and neck** and has the child been **immunised against mumps?**

YES — **ADVICE** It is probably swollen glands. Give the child paracetamol and ask your pharmacist for advice. **If it continues for a week, speak to your doctor.**

NO

Is there also **earache?**

YES — See **Earache**
ADVICE Middle ear infections may be the culprit. **Call your doctor and give paracetamol to ease the pain.**

NO

Is there a **sore throat** or **sneezing** or **a cough** or **a runny nose?**

YES — See **Colds and flu**
ADVICE It is probably a cold or flu. Ask your pharmacist for advice.

NO

Is there also **diarrhoea?**

YES — **ADVICE** Babies and children lose water very quickly. **Call your doctor** but also check **Diarrhoea.**

NO

Is there any **difficulty in breathing?**

YES — **ADVICE** Any difficulty in breathing in children for whatever cause needs medical attention. **Call your doctor** but also see **Breathing difficulties.**

NO

Is there **pain in the tummy (abdomen)?**

YES — **ADVICE** There are many reasons why children will have abdominal pain and thankfully most of them are not serious. Even so check out **Abdominal pain.**

NO

Is the child **difficult to wake** or **not talking** or **not keeping down fluids** or **complaining of the light hurting their eyes?**

YES — **ADVICE** As it can be difficult to be sure whether you are dealing with something simple or serious, you should check with the section on **Meningitis** and **ring your doctor.**

NO

Is there **a rash?**

YES — **ADVICE** Rashes often accompany a fever. Check out the section on **Rashes with fever.**

NO

Self care advice
- Give the child regular paracetamol to reduce the temperature (check the instructions on the packet for the right dose).
- Give them an extra amount of their favourite drink or ice lollies.
- Make sure the child is not over dressed - a vest and nappy/pants is enough clothing for them as long as the house is at the normal room temperature.
- Cover the child in a light cotton sheet when in bed.
- If the condition gets worse or new symptoms develop, **call your doctor.**

PART 9 Miscellaneous

Congenital heart disease

Few things worry parents more than congenital defects in their child's heart. Unfortunately they are not rare, affecting about one baby in 120. Being congenital, they are by definition present from birth, but many not be diagnosed until later on when symptoms such as breathing problems first arise.

It would be easy to get very upset over this issue, but it is worth remembering that most defects will cause no problem to the child and the remainder can often be treated successfully so that they have a normal or near-normal life. Many children will grow into healthy adults without ever realising there is a congenital defect in their heart which has never caused a problem and so was never diagnosed as such. Even the term, 'a hole in the heart' raises the spectre of some sort of gap in the outside wall of the heart rather like a punctured inner tube. Simply understanding the actual way the heart is affected can help reassure.

Congenital heart disease take several forms. The commonest are:

● Openings in the internal wall of the heart ('hole in the heart'). These are called septal defects as the septum separates the two sides of the heart.
● Persistence of a blood channel used only while the baby is in the womb which should close off after birth. This is called patent ductus arteriosus (PDA).
● Narrowing of the main artery of the body, the aorta. This is called aortic stenosis.
● Narrowing of the main heart valves. This is called aortic and pulmonary valve stenosis.
● A complex of all four defects occurring together. This is called Fallot's tetralogy.

All of these defects vary enormously in severity but result in a mixing of oxygenated blood from the lungs with deoxygenated blood returning from the rest of the body. Deoxygenated blood is blue/red in colour while oxygenated blood is bright red. The heart normally keeps them separate, giving the body a pink colour. When they mix, places like the lips especially turn slightly blue, which is made worse when oxygen is in higher demand.

Symptoms

A common symptom is cyanosis, a bluish skin colour especially around the lips, and sufferers are breathless and easily tired. Varying levels of activity can bring this on, along with a characteristic squatting position during recovery. Most murmurs, noises in the heart as blood is being pumped, are innocent but if there is a congenital defect the characteristic murmur can often be heard using a stethoscope.

Causes

Parents often feel guilty, that they somehow brought on the problem in some way. In truth there are many different causes of congenital heart disease:

● Virus infections early in pregnancy, especially German measles (rubella). It is vital that both boys and girls are vaccinated against this infection.
● Some medical drugs, taken in the early weeks of pregnancy. The dreadful Thalidomide tragedy is thankfully very rare. Very few medicines cause harm but all medicines should only be taken under medical advice during pregnancy.
● Some poorly-controlled medical conditions in the mother such as diabetes or Systemic Lupus Erythematosus (SLE). These conditions are treatable during pregnancy and often improve, but more importantly any potential damage to the baby can be minimised by careful monitoring and control.
● Down's syndrome unfortunately may include congenital heart defects, but like the severity of the condition itself, varies enormously between children.

Diagnosis

Generally it is usually the parent who first raises the alarm after seeing a bluish tinge in the skin and breathlessness. Referral to a paediatrician will result in further tests such as a chest X-ray, electrocardiograms (ECG: this picks up electrical activity from the heart), echocardiography (ultrasound to look at how the valves are working) and possibly the passage of fine tubes into the heart (cardiac catheterisation to see where and how the blood is mixing).

Prevention

Most of the problems cannot be prevented other than addressing causes such as uncontrolled medical conditions, avoiding drugs especially during early pregnancy and ensuring immunity from German measles before becoming pregnant.

Complications

Thankfully, modern surgery reduces the complications to a minimum but otherwise there can be poor growth, thickening (clubbing) of the tips of the fingers and toes, poor ability to remain active, chest and possibly other infections and a danger of the heart itself being infected.

Treatment

Surgical correction of the congenital defect is often advised during infancy or childhood. Often this will involve two stages, the last being performed when the child is older. All children will benefit from treatment and most will have normal or near-normal lives so it is important to alert your doctor or health visitor to any problems such as breathlessness or blue colouration of the lips.

Febrile convulsions

Febrile convulsions are quite common in young children, but the great majority of children who suffer these episodes are not epileptic and these fits do not occur because of any brain defect, nor do they mean that the child will develop epilepsy in future. High body temperature is invariably the cause.

Around 3 or 4 children out of 1000 will have a febrile convulsion by the time they are five years old. In most cases the fits occur after the age of six months; they typically occur between the ages of 6 months and 6 years.

Symptoms

Febrile convulsions seldom last for longer than a few minutes, and although the child may take a few minutes to recover, their final recovery is complete.

Causes

Conditions commonly causing fevers include middle ear infection (otitis media), tonsillitis, kidney or urinary infection, pneumonia and any of the common infectious diseases of childhood such as measles, mumps, chicken pox and whooping cough. Even the common cold or flu can be a trigger.

Any illness causing a temperature higher than 39°C (102.2°F) can set off a febrile convulsion.

Diagnosis

If the convulsions cease when the child's temperature drops this gives an obvious diagnosis, but they should still be reported to your doctor.

Prevention

High temperatures can be brought down with simple things like cooling the room, removing clothing and tepid sponging (using a flannel or sponge to apply tepid water which then evaporates, cooling the child). Medicines such as paediatric ibuprofen, paracetamol liquid medicine or paracetamol suppositories (tablets that you place inside the child's bottom) will also help. Any seizure for whatever cause should be reported to your doctor, although you may not always need a visit.

Complications

Injury from hitting hard objects is a possibility and prolonged seizures due to high temperature can cause brain damage.

Umbilical hernia

There are often things that can happen to a baby which appear serious but which are common, sort themselves out or can be treated very easily. Umbilical hernias are a good example.

Symptoms

A bulge is seen or felt close to the belly button which is soft but not painful. It can often disappear on its own only to return a few days later.

Causes

For a while after being born, the muscle layer around the belly button (umbilicus) can be weak or even have a small gap in it. Not surprisingly, some of the inside of the abdomen can protrude through causing a 'hernia'. This can range from a small amount of fatty tissue to part of the intestine itself. Umbilical hernias are most likely to appear in the first three weeks of life as your baby's belly button heals up after the birth and they are twice as common in boys as in girls. Anything which increases the pressure inside the abdomen such as crying, laughing, or coughing can make the hernia appear larger.

Treatment

Fortunately the majority of umbilical hernias correct themselves by two to three years old but occasionally surgery is needed after this age to strengthen the area around the tummy button and hold in the bulge. Most doctors prefer to wait and see if the hernia gets larger after the first year or resolves itself. Generally, doctors will only recommend surgery if the hernia hasn't gone away by three years old or progressively worsens in the first few years.

Self care

It is worth keeping an eye on any bulge around your baby's umbilical cord stump (newborns) or tummy button (older babies and toddlers). If it feels hot, changes colour (especially blue) or is tender you must phone your doctor. If the child is passing blood in their motions or vomiting repeatedly you must call 999/112.

The hernia should be disappearing by the age of 2, so if it is still there ask your doctor's advice.

Shock (loss of blood)

Children in shock may become pale, sweaty, drowsy and confused. They need urgent medical attention. While waiting for help, remain calm but do not give them anything to eat or drink. If they are unconscious lie them on their back with their legs raised, loosen any tight clothing and keep them warm.

Reference

Medical records

Illnesses . . . .

Allergies . . . .

Accidents . . . .

Other problems . . . .

. . . .

. . . .

. . . .

Contact details

GP . . . .

Health visitor . . . .

Hospital . . . .

Dentist . . . .

Nursery or playgroup . . . .

Childminder . . . .

Babysitter . . . .

Others . . . .

. . . .

. . . .

. . . .

Contacts

Alcoholics anonymous
Tel 0845 769 7555
www.alcoholics-anonymous.org.uk

Breastfeeding line
Tel 0870 444 8708
9am-6pm

The British Red Cross
Tel 0870 170 7000
www.redcross.org.uk

Children's Information Service (CIS)
Gives details about pre-schools near where
you live.
Tel: 0800 96 02 96 (Freephone)
www.childcarelink.gov.uk

Community Hygiene Concern
Tel 020 7686 4321
www.chc.org

**Cot Death helpline (The Foundation for the
Study of Infant Deaths)**
Tel 020 7233 2090
Mon-Fri 9am-11pm,
Sat-Sun 6pm-11pm
www.sids.org.uk

Department of Health
PO Box 777, London SE1 6XH

Directgov
www.direct.gov.uk

Drinkline
Tel 0800 917 8282
www.patient.co.uk
www.wrecked.co.uk

Epilepsy Action
0808 800 5050
www.epilepsy.org.uk

Family Planning Association
Tel 0845 122 8690
Mon-Fri 9am-6pm
www.fpa.org.uk

Inland Revenue
www.hmrc.gov.uk

MENCAP
123 Golden Lane
London EC1Y 0RT
020 7454 0454
020 7608 3254
information@mencap.org.uk
www.mencap.org.uk

The Meningitis Research Foundation
Tel 080 8800 3344
www.meningitis.org

The Meningitis Trust
Tel 0800 028 18 28
www.meningitis-trust.org

Men's Health Forum
Websites:
www.malehealth.co.uk (UK)
www.mhfs.org.uk (Scotland)
www.mhfi.org (Ireland)
www.emhf.org (Europe)

NHS Direct
Tel 0845 46 47
www.nhsdirect.nhs.uk

Ofsted
For school inspection reports.
www.ofsted.gov.uk

The Prevention and Treatment of Head Lice
Tel 020 7210 4850
9am-5pm
www.dh.gov.uk

Quitline
Tel 0800 00 22 00
www.quit.org.uk

Raising kids
Tel 0208 444 4852
www.raisingkids.co.uk

Relate
www.relate.org.uk

**Sexual Health Direct (Run by the Family
Planning Association)**
Tel 0845 122 8690
Mon-Fri 9am-6pm
www.fpa.org.uk

St John Ambulance
Tel 08700 10 49 50
www.st-john-ambulance.org.uk

Working Families
Tel 0800 013 0313
www.workingfamilies.org.uk

Credits

Toddlers	Augusta, Freya, Sophia and Eddie
Cover design	Pete Shoemark
Editor	Ian Barnes
Editorial director	Matthew Minter
Page build	James Robertson
Technical illustrations	Mark Stevens and Matthew Marke
Photography	All photos are from istockphoto.com, except Paul Tanswell (page 109), J Haynes (cover and pages 11, 26, 29, 70, 81, 117 and 135), Valencia Haynes (pages 23 and 120) and Marc Haynes (page 69)
Production control	Charles Seaton